D0341029

THE
COMPENDIUM
OF

AMAZING
GARDENING
INNOVATIONS

ABIGAIL WILLIS

Illustrations by Dave Hopkins

LAURENCE KING PUBLISHING

FOR MUTTI

Published in 2018 by
Laurence King Publishing
361–373 City Road
London EC1V 1LR
United Kingdom
T +44 20 7841 6900
F +44 20 7841 6910
enquiries@laurenceking.com
www.laurenceking.com

A catalogue record for this book is available from the
British Library.

ISBN: 978 1 78627 317 8

33614080807026

Design concept: John Dowling
Design: Rosa Nussbaum

Printed in China

CONTENTS

INTRODUCTION

How does your garden grow? Does it have a lawn, edged by borders abundant with colourful cottage plants and fragrant roses? Perhaps you have banned colour entirely, opting for a sophisticated palette of ghostly white blooms that glow like moonlight in the fading light of a summer's day. Or have you ditched your labour-intensive lawn in favour of an eco-friendly dry garden, or a fashionable swathe of prairie plants?

Or maybe you've fallen for tender exotics – beautiful but requiring the warm embrace of a heated greenhouse. Or are vegetables more your bag, grown in decorative rows in a kitchen garden or laid out in workmanlike lines on an allotment? You may well have given up on digging too, tending your garden on organic principles and steering clear of synthetic pesticides and weedkillers.

And when you're not gardening, no doubt you're mugging up about it (gardening is an addictive and absorbing pastime!), poring over glossy magazines and seed catalogues, checking out the latest trends and expert advice on seasonal jobs in the garden.

So many of these things were once novelties, the result of technological or aesthetic innovation. The impact of nineteenth-century inventions such as Dr Ward's case and Mr Budding's lawnmower is still being felt in the twenty-first century, influencing the plants we grow as well as the way we manage them, while some – water features and topiary, for example – have been with us for hundreds, if not thousands, of years.

And when it comes to garden design, perhaps it can be said that there is nothing truly new under the sun. Over the centuries, garden design has evolved through alternating cycles of formality and more naturalistic styles, each reincarnation reinventing its predecessor in a slightly different way. The ebb and flow of fashion is as inevitable in horticulture as it is in hemlines.

This miscellany celebrates 50 of gardening's greatest ideas – a potted history, as it were, of the everyday things we take for granted in our gardening lives.

Abigail Willis
Somerset
November 2017

THE WARDIAN CASE

Like the storm in a petri dish that became the wonder drug penicillin, the **WARDIAN CASE** *was the product of an* **ACCIDENTAL DISCOVERY** *in a glass jar that would go on to have* **GLOBAL SIGNIFICANCE.**

Nathaniel Bagshaw Ward was a doctor with a passion for botany and natural history that the smog and pollution of his East London home could not extinguish. In around 1829, while attempting to raise a hawk moth in a sealed glass bottle, Dr Ward discovered that a grass seed and a fern had germinated in the damp leaf mould in which he had placed the moth chrysalis. The moth having pupated successfully, Ward's volunteer plants lived on for several years in their enclosed environment, indifferent to seasonal temperature changes, sustained by the cycle of evaporation and condensation of water within the jar and protected from the noxious London smog that kept killing off Ward's beloved collection of native ferns in his back garden.

Intrigued, Ward set about experimenting in earnest. Assisted by one of the leading nurseries of the day, Loddiges of Hoxton, two 'Ward's cases' were packed with plants and dispatched to Sydney in 1833. Having survived the long voyage, the cases were repacked with Australian specimens such as *Gleichenia microphylla* (scrambling coral fern) and returned to England where they (and a few opportunistic *Callicona serrata*, or black wattle, seedlings that had germinated en voyage) arrived at Loddiges the following year in 'the most healthy and vigorous condition'. They had not been watered during the eight-month trip and had withstood temperatures on deck ranging from –7 to 49°C (20 to 120°F).

Plant collectors lost no time in exploiting this new technology. Prior to the Wardian case, the survival rate of plants on a long sea voyage was a dismal 1 in 20; now a survival rate of 19 out of 20 was possible. New plant introductions proliferated, and an international plant trade boomed. In 1841 Joseph Hooker used a 1.2-metre (4-foot)-long Ward's case to ship plants from New Zealand to his father, William Jackson Hooker, the director of Kew Gardens. His selection included ferns such as *Doodia caudata* and the greenhood orchid *Pterosylis banksii*. In America, Dr George Rogers Hall's mid-nineteenth-century introductions of Japanese plants such as the umbrella pine, the ornamental crab apple (*Malus halliana*) and *Magnolia stellata* all came courtesy of the Wardian case.

Ward envisaged a philanthropic use for his invention – he thought that the urban poor could use his cases for growing healthy salads. Instead it became a powerful empire-building tool, the means by which, in 1848, Robert Fortune was able to transport thousands of tea plants from China to inaugurate the tea trade in India. And it was instrumental in the introduction of quinine-bearing cinchona trees from South America to the sub-continent, and

Brazilian rubber trees to Malaya (via Kew). The last shipment of plants to Kew Gardens in a Wardian case came from Fiji in 1962.

While sturdy wood-and-glass Wardian cases were criss-crossing the high seas, ornamental metal-and-glass versions filled with the fruits of many a plant-hunting expedition rapidly colonized the living rooms of the botanically minded middle classes. Resembling scaled-down greenhouses or even mini palm houses, and also available as DIY kits, these decorative terrariums allowed householders of even quite modest means to participate in the great fern and orchid crazes of the nineteenth century that had been pioneered by aristocratic plant collectors. In this, at least, the cases performed a function as egalitarian as Ward had first intended.

THE
LAWNMOWER

A VELVET-SMOOTH LAWN
is the **HOLY GRAIL** *for many gardeners,*
so it is fitting that the inspiration for the **FIRST**
LAWNMOWER *should have come from the*
TEXTILE INDUSTRY.

In 1830, Gloucestershire engineer Edwin Beard Budding was the man who spotted that a new-fangled cylinder cross-cutting machine used to trim the nap of woollen cloth could be adapted for grass-shaving duties.

Budding developed his design with John Ferrabee at the Phoenix Iron Works and a patent for their lawnmower, the world's first, was issued in August 1830, specifying 'a new combination and application of machinery for the purpose of cropping or shearing the vegetable surface of lawns, grass-plats and pleasure grounds'.

Prior to Budding's invention, what might be termed 'recreational grass' was kept in trim by grazing livestock or the scythe. Both options were a rich man's game; the former suitable for Capability Brown-style parkland in which attractive clusters of sheep or cows were part of the Arcadian fantasy, the latter requiring frequent mowing sessions by teams of scythe-wielding mowers. Adjusting the height of the cut was achieved by attaching wooden blocks to the mowers' shoes (a refinement not available, presumably, to the cows).

Made of cast iron, Budding's lawnmowers featured a rear roller and gear wheels but were heavy to use. They nonetheless found a ready market (Regent's Park Zoological Gardens and Oxford colleges were early customers), and when the patents were relaxed in the 1850s competitors were quick to market improved versions. Notable among these was the 'Silens Messor', manufactured by Thomas Green of Leeds. This light and easy-to-manoeuvre 'silent cutter' used a chain drive as opposed to Budding's gear drive, and was available in a range of mowing widths, the larger of which could be pulled by horse, pony or donkey. It was still being manufactured into the 1930s.

Steam, petrol and electric variants followed at intervals from the 1890s, and in 1965 the hovercraft-inspired Flymo came on the scene. More recently, the mower family has been joined by propane- and solar-powered 'eco' models, but the die had long been cast: a neatly trimmed lawn was as achievable (and desirable) for the middling sorts as it was for the gentry, with lawns becoming a ubiquitous feature of the nineteenth-century suburban villa garden. Lawn-based pastimes such as croquet and tennis took off and, like the games themselves, the very activity of mowing was promoted as a healthful pursuit for both sexes.

In America, the desirability of 'grass mown into softness like velvet' was extolled by landscape designer Andrew Jackson Downing, a pastoral vision continued by his protégés Calvert Vaux and Frederick Law Olmsted. In the 1860s, Olmsted's design for the suburb of Riverside, Illinois, established the template for millions of subsequent American front lawns, with houses set back from the road and no fences to interrupt the grass apron between dwelling and highway. Somewhere along the line, tidy lawns became equated with moral rectitude; in the 'Levittown' suburban developments of the 1950s, strictly enforced covenants required residents to maintain their front lawns, their creator Abraham Levitt being of the view that 'a fine carpet of green grass stamps the inhabitants as good neighbors, as desirable citizens'.

ARTS & CRAFTS GARDENS

Combining **INFORMAL** *cottage planting with* **FORMAL** *structure and a hint of* **FADED ITALIAN GRANDEUR**, *the Arts and Crafts garden was the* **QUINTESSENTIAL ENGLISH** *garden style of the twentieth century.*

Arts and Crafts gardens retain their mass appeal in the twenty-first century, as exemplified in the restoration of the Hampstead Pergola. First created between 1905 and 1925 – at the height of the first vogue for the Arts and Crafts style – it was part of the extensive gardens of Lord Leverhulme's home in northwest London. The city subsequently purchased it for the public in a very neglected state. In the late 1990s, work began to restore it in the spirit of the Arts and Crafts style, successfully mixing the formal and informal to achieve a kind of elegance that is simultaneously welcoming and self assured.

From their very first conception, Arts and Crafts gardens were a reaction against the unrelenting formality of High Victorian gardens. The style took its name from the 1900 publication *The Art & Craft of Garden Making*, by Thomas Mawson.

Proponents of the style, Gertrude Jekyll, Vita Sackville-West and the doyenne of cottage plants, Margery Fish, all wrote persuasively about their own gardens, enthusing a wide audience through their books and journalism. 'Profusion, even extravagance and exuberance, within confines of the utmost linear severity', was how Sackville-West's de-

scribed her garden at Sissinghurst Castle and she also opened Sissinghurst to the public at a shilling per head.

This relaxed approach to planting can, in fact, trace its roots back to the combative Irish garden writer William Robinson, whose 1870 book *The Wild Garden* put the case for an easy-going naturalism using hardy perennials that was at odds with the geometric displays of tender bedding plants then prevalent in English Victorian gardens.

Extolling the 'charm and simplicity' of cottage gardens, Robinson promoted his vision through his magazines, whose like-minded contributors included William Morris and Gertrude Jekyll. Morris's garden at the Red House was, as might be expected from the founding father of the Arts and Crafts movement, a prototypically Arts and Crafts garden, not only for its old-fashioned flowers and fruit trees but also for the way in which it explicitly related to the medieval styling of the house.

Gertrude Jekyll's writing established her reputation as a colourist and plantswoman. Informed by her training as an artist, Jekyll's sure sense of colour harmonics elevated the mixed border into an art form. Her 1908 book *Colour Schemes for the Flower Garden* became a seminal text, offering guidance on how to achieve the classic Jekyllian cool-to-hot-to-cool colour progression in the border.

Jekyll's fruitful collaboration with the architect Edwin Lutyens (which began in 1889, when the latter was just 26) consolidated the Arts and Crafts garden's integration of house and garden, as well as its vocabulary of pergolas, rills, sunken lawns, and dry stone walls brimming with Mexican fleabane.

Despite their air of domestic tranquillity, Arts and Crafts gardens were hotly contested territory in their day, with William Robinson arguing for informality, and the architect Reginald Blomfield championing formality. Their differences were not, in fact, irreconcilable: Robinson's own garden at Gravetye Manor had its fair share of straight lines, while Blomfield's at Point Hill had none. Robinson was wrong about one thing, though. This way of gardening was anything but low maintenance: the best Arts and Crafts gardens were (and are) lifelong labours of love.

ROSES

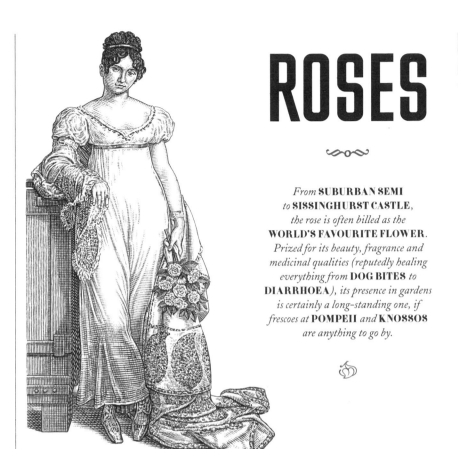

From **SUBURBAN SEMI**
to **SISSINGHURST CASTLE**,
the rose is often billed as the
WORLD'S FAVOURITE FLOWER.
*Prized for its beauty, fragrance and
medicinal qualities (reputedly healing
everything from* **DOG BITES** *to*
DIARRHOEA), *its presence in gardens
is certainly a long-standing one, if
frescoes at* **POMPEII** *and* **KNOSSOS**
are anything to go by.

From the seventeenth century, the rose became the centre of a breeding obsession when Dutch nurserymen strove to perfect the centifolia (many-petalled) rose. The centifolia's genealogy is hazy, but it is believed to be a cross between the gallica rose (an ancient European species) and the damask rose (reputedly introduced to Europe by returning Crusaders).

The arrival of 'China tea roses' in the late eighteenth and early nineteenth centuries, brought repeat-flowering, strongly coloured, scented blooms into the nurseries (up until this points the only repeating, or remontant, rose in Europe had been the 'autumn damask'). Four stud roses, including 'Parson's Pink China' and 'Hume's Blush Tea-Scented China', were sent to Europe between 1792 and 1824, and became the foundation of hundreds of new varieties.

Rose breeders were kept busy in particular by the empress Joséphine Bonaparte, who made it her mission to collect every known variety of rose. By the time of her death in 1814, her innovative rose garden at the Château de Malmaison contained some 250 varieties. *Les Roses*, a magisterial three-volume record of Joséphine's roses, was published by the botanical artist Redouté after her death, further cementing her legacy to rosiculture. Rose gardens soon became fashionable – one of the most famous being the roseraie at L'Haÿ, near Paris, established in 1914.

The pre-eminence of the French breeders resulted in the breakthrough introduction in 1867 of 'La France', the first hybrid tea rose. A cross between a tea rose and a hybrid perpetual, the hybrid tea is characterized by pointed buds, long upright stems and vibrant colours. Not regarded as good mixers, and prone to disease, hybrid teas were traditionally grouped together in separate rose beds. The twentieth century's bestselling rose was 'Peace', a French-bred hybrid tea originally called 'Mme A. Meilland', which was spirited to safety in America on the eve of World War II, and released under its new name in 1945.

Thanks to breeders, there is a rose for every aspiration and aspect. Romantic swags of climbing and rambling roses festoon the pillars and pergolas of Arts and Crafts-style gardens, and in the Cotswolds the empire-building 'Kiftsgate' rambler extends to 25 metres (82 feet), but not every garden can accommodate such largesse. In the 1970s and 80s, breeders developed robust 'patio' and 'miniature' roses for small modern gardens, while nurseries in Scandinavia and North America have focused on traits such as winter hardiness. At the same time in Britain, rose expert Graham Stuart Thomas revived interest in 'old' roses, while David Austin began developing his 'English' roses, which combine the informal charm of old roses with disease resistance, fragrance and repeat flowering, and associate well in mixed borders.

SECATEURS

Allegedly inspired by the **GUILLOTINE**, *secateurs were invented by the French aristocrat Marquis* **BERTRAND DE MOLEVILLE** *in around 1815. His device appropriately proved equally adept at* **DEADHEADING** *and* **PRECISION PRUNING.**

An indispensable bit of kit for most gardeners, secateurs were not an instant hit when they first appeared in the first half of the nineteenth century. Before then, pruning was done with billhooks and pruning knifes, tools that had been used for millennia, arriving in Europe, like so many other things, via Ancient Egypt, Greece and the Roman

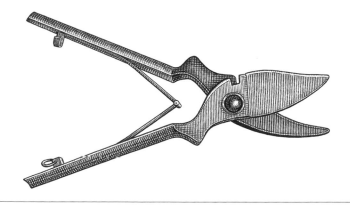

Empire. Given this long lineage, it was perhaps not surprising that there was resistance in some quarters to the new-fangled secateurs.

The first mention of secateurs appears to have been in 1819, in the French almanac *Le Bon Jardinier*. Although they eventually became the pruning tool of choice for vignerons across France, de Moleville's nifty shears clearly took a little getting used to. Their tendency to crush stems when used incorrectly did not endear them to professional growers, although proper usage was explained in Philibert Baron's 1858 fruit-pruning manual, *Nouveaux principes de taille des arbres fruitiers*.

Gardening writers on both sides of the Channel promoted the secateur to amateur and professional gardeners alike. The French horticulturalist, fruit expert and editor Pierre-Antoine Poiteau was an enthusiast, while by as early as 1825 gardening journalist John Claudius Loudon was recommending 'French pruning-shears' to English readers as an 'expeditious implement for pruning the vine' in his *Encyclopaedia of Gardening*.

William Robinson was also a convert. Having seen secateurs in action in France, he jettisoned his pruning knife, writing in his 1869 book *The Parks, Promenades and Gardens*

of Paris, 'There can be no doubt that where much pruning of any kind is done, and particularly pruning of a rather rough nature, the secateur is a valuable instrument'.

Although early designs were often equipped with unwieldy integral billhooks (old habits really did die hard), de Moleville's invention evolved into an efficient tool. Bypass and anvil secateurs are the two main variations on the theme: the former have a sharpened upper blade that slides alongside the lower blade, while anvil secateurs have an upper blade that cuts in a crushing action by coming down onto a lower blade. Twentieth-century innovations have included rotating handles and ergonomic shapes, and niceties such as wire-cutting notches and left-handed versions.

Loudon may have sniffily noted gardeners' 'superstitious attachment' to their pruning knives, but modern secateurs inspire equal devotion. Some swear by the Swiss company Felco, which launched its classic red-handled bypass secateur in 1948; others will not be parted from their ergonomic Swedish Bahco pruning shears, designed for professional horticulturalists who make between 5,000 and 12,000 pruning cuts a day – a figure that puts the task of pruning the average garden into perspective.

FAIRCHILD'S MULE

Hard to imagine now, Hoxton in northeast London
was once a **HORTICULTURAL HOTSPOT**, known for
its nurseries and market gardens rather than its hipsters.
In 1717 it was the scene of one of modern gardening's
MOST SIGNIFICANT developments: the creation of
Europe's **FIRST MAN-MADE HYBRID PLANT**.

Thomas Fairchild was the man in question, a practical nurseryman with a particular skill for raising and nurturing introductions from the New World. Fairchild was also, to use the contemporary phrase, 'curious', and his enquiring mind led him to see what would happen if he placed (male) pollen from a sweet william (*Dianthus barbatus*) into the (female) pistil of a carnation (*D. caryophyllus*). The resultant seeds produced a plant, new to nature, that somewhat resembled each of its parents and provided the first proof of the theory that plants reproduced sexually.

Thanks to its first-generation hybrid vigour, *Dianthus barbatus x caryophyllus* flowered its socks off for months on end, but was unable to produce viable seed (hence the 'Mule' sobriquet). Up until this moment, the only way nurserymen could widen the choice of plants available to their customers was by selecting naturally occurring crosses and sports, and propagating them by cuttings. Fairchild's discovery that it was possible to breed plants selectively would, in due course, pave the way for an epidemic of plant breeding in the following century, but in his own religiously conservative day, contradicting the orthodoxy that all of nature was created by God was a risky business. Fairchild's unease in the matter (or perhaps simply his

innate modesty) can be inferred from the absence of any mention of the Mule in his own writings, and his endowment of an annual sermon on the subject of 'the Wonderful World of God in the Creation' by way of atonement.

By the nineteenth century, such scruples seemed less pressing; indeed, it was a Roman Catholic cleric, Gregor Johann Mendel, whose mid-century experiments hybridizing peas established the concept of dominant and recessive genes. Nurserymen were also busy filling their catalogues with glamorous new varieties of irises, orchids, dahlias, chrysanthemums, roses, fuchsias and water lilies. The nursery of French horticulturalist Victor Lemoine alone introduced some 153 named lilac cultivars between 1876 and 1927 (although Lemoine's poor eyesight meant it was the long-suffering Madame Lemoine who actually did the painstaking work of hand pollination; Lemoine did at least name a magnificent double white lilac in her honour). All these, along with much-loved twentieth-century introductions such as Benton irises (created by the painter Cedric Morris), Russell lupins, Spencer sweet peas and David Austin's roses are all, in their way, descendants of the Mule – the sterile plant that proved so richly fertile.

PLANT HUNTERS

For an occupation usually regarded as sedate, gardening has a surprisingly **SWASHBUCKLING** *hinterland.* *Gardeners have long* **LUSTED OVER** *exotic plants, and for centuries plant hunters have travelled the globe, braving all kinds of* **DANGERS***, to procure* **NEW SPECIMENS** *– sometimes, as in the case of Meriwether Lewis and William Clark's* 1804–6 **EXPEDITION** *across America for Thomas Jefferson, quite literally charting* **NEW TERRITORY** *as they botanized.*

Lewis and Clark at least made it home (having discovered such garden-worthy treasures as *Philadelphus lewisii* and *Clarkia pulchella*). The story of plant hunting is otherwise littered with corpses, catastrophes and pitfalls of the most literal kind.

Robert Fortune's exploits on behalf of the Royal Horticultural Society included fighting pirates, smuggling tea plants out of China, contracting malaria and dangling over a boar pit. David Douglas (he of the fir) was not so 'Fortunate'; having botanized successfully across America, he met an untimely end in 1834, aged just 35, at the bottom of a wild bullock trap in Hawaii. French missionary and botanist Père Jean-Marie Delavay was felled by bubonic plague in the plant-rich territory of Yunnan in 1895, but not before bequeathing the blue poppy *Meconopsis betonicifolia* to Western gardeners. Modern-day planters do not have it much easier: in 2000 Tom Hart Dyke spent nine months in captivity, having been kidnapped while searching for orchids in the Panamanian jungle. Douglas and Delavay may not have made old bones, but their names, like those of other plant collectors, live on in plants such as *Quercus douglasii* and *Paeonia delavayi*.

The earliest recorded plant-hunting expedition was instigated by the pharaoh Hatshepsut in 1500 BC and successfully relocated a number of frankincense trees from the African Land of Punt to the queen's funerary garden. Relief carvings show how the highly prized specimens were transported, root ball and all, to their new home in Egypt.

Later plant-hunting sponsors included not just royals and statesmen but also churchmen like Bishop Compton (whose garden at Fulham Palace was the first in Britain to contain a *Magnolia virginiana*, retrieved from Virginia for him by the missionary Reverend Banister), nurseries such as Veitch, and scientific institutions including the Jardin des Plantes in Paris and Kew Gardens in London. Kew's first official plant hunter was Francis Masson, whose expedition to South Africa in the 1770s

introduced over 40 species of *Pelargonium*. The *Encephalartos altensteinii* cycad brought back by Masson to Kew in 1775 flourishes still: the world's oldest pot plant.

Swedish plant hunter Carl Peter Thunberg spent three years in South Africa learning Dutch in order to botanize in Japan in 1775 as part of the Dutch East India Company (the only organization at the time allowed access to the archipelago). His dedication paid off: in the Cape Thunberg was the first Westerner to describe the red tea bush (*Aspalathus linearis*), while in Japan his many discoveries included that stalwart provider of autumnal colour, *Acer palmatum*.

Empire builders or champions of biodiversity (the choice is yours), plant hunters have changed the way our gardens look, from the towering monkey puzzle trees beloved of the Victorians (the first specimens of which came to Britain in 1795 via Archibald Menzies, who retrieved the seeds having been served the cones for dinner in Chile) to the early twentieth-century craze for rock gardening inspired by Reginald Farrer's single-minded quest for alpine plants mountains near and far.

CHEMICAL GARDENING

There is no denying it, gardening can be **HARD WORK***; its long history of* **DIGGING, WEEDING, MANURING** *and* **MANICURING** *is recorded in the stooped figures who labour in medieval psalters, and in sepia photographs of the serried ranks of gardeners tending the grounds of wealthy Victorians. To* **MAXIMIZE PRODUCTIVITY***, the use of* **CHEMICALS** *in horticulture became* **WIDESPREAD** *from the nineteenth century.*

The gardener's need for fertile soil and desire to control weeds, pests and diseases is a perennial challenge, but over the years gardeners discovered that chemicals could save time and labour. The Victorians' murderous penchant for arsenic extended to horticulture, where it was used as an insecticide and rat poison, and in agriculture, where it was used for large-scale campaigns such as the 'tiger moth wars' in the US.

The militaristic analogy was apt; many of the chemicals in the twentieth century gardener's arsenal also served in the two world wars. Fritz Haber's 1909 process for synthesizing nitrogen made possible the mass manufacturing of nitrate fertilizers (whose explosive qualities were also harnessed by the munitions industry). By the end of World War II, the US was the world's largest producer of nitrogen, and in peacetime, production output switched from weapons to huge quantities of fertilizer. Yields increased, as did weeds and pests, but no matter: the war effort had also seen the arrival of potent insecticides such as the anti-malarial DDT (patented in 1940), organophosphates (developed as nerve agents), along with herbicides such as 2,4-D (an ingredient of the defoliant Agent Orange).

Where agriculture led, horticulture followed, and for a while in the mid-twentieth century it seemed as if chemicals might also provide gardeners with a silver bullet. Seductive advertising extolled the ease and efficacy of products, encouraging a generation of trigger-happy gardeners to reach for the spray.

It was, predictably, all too good to be true. *Silent Spring*, Rachel Carson's 1962 exposé of the environmental hazards of DDT, led to a US government investigation into its safety, followed by a ban there in 1972. Despite the ensuing scepticism about the wisdom of using toxic chemicals in gardens and in food production, chemical gardening has proved

a hard habit to break. An EU directive on pesticides in 2002 resulted in over 80 garden products being withdrawn from sale, drawing howls of protest from gardeners (including the world's bestselling gardening author Dr D. G. Hessayon). At the time of writing, the weedkiller glyphosate and neonicotinoid insecticides are under scrutiny.

Even before the new millennium, 'chemical gardening' was beginning to look out of touch. The 'integrated pest management' approach, developed in the wake of *Silent Spring*, prioritizes physical barriers, hand and biological controls over chemical intervention, a pragmatism that is echoed in the UK by the RHS, which advises that 'non-chemical means of control are always the first choice'. By now, many gardeners had already made up their own minds and had switched to organic methods, their ranks including high-profile figures such as the Prince of Wales, and the BBC's gardener Geoff Hamilton, whose *Organic Garden Book* was published in 1987.

ORGANIC GARDENING

Before they became **WEAPONIZED** *with chemical fertilizers,* **PESTICIDES** *and* **HERBICIDES**, *most gardeners were 'organic' by necessity.* **ORGANIC GARDENING** *as a lifestyle choice grew out of its agricultural counterpart, which emerged in response to the rise of* **AGRI-CHEMICALS** *after World War I.*

In northern Europe, Rudolf Steiner's ideas about the 'spiritual foundation' of agriculture, expounded in 1924, developed into biodynamic agriculture, an approach to farming that avoided chemicals (but whose more esoteric practices were derided, even in organic circles, as 'muck and magic').

Among the organic movement's champions in the UK was Lady Eve Balfour, author of *The Living Soil*, whose decades-long experiments at her farm in Haughley, Suffolk, tested the merits of organic farming, and resulted in the establishment of the Soil Association in 1946. Following Lady Balfour's lead in the US, farmer and publisher J. I. Rodale set up his eponymous Institute in 1947 to research and promote organic practices, further spreading the word to gardeners via his magazine *Organic Farming and Gardening* (later *Organic Gardening*; now *Rodale's Organic Life*).

Soil health lies at the heart of organic growing, and much research was carried out into natural ways of maintaining soil vitality. Sir Albert Howard, whose study of traditional Indian farming in the 1920s evolved into the 'Indore method' of composting agricultural waste materials, was a notable pioneer. In Britain, Lawrence Hills experimented with Russian comfrey as a crop and fertilizer, and in 1954 he founded the Henry Doubleday Research Association to promote organic gardening. The HDRA (named after the nineteenth-century nurseryman who introduced Russian comfrey into the UK) is now the charity Garden Organic which in addition to maintaining demonstration gardens at Ryton near Coventry runs a 'Master Composter' programme, educating householders in the art of composting.

A preoccupation with compost runs like a rich, dark seam of humus through the story of organic gardening. Dr W. E. Shewell-Cooper, the founder of another British organic gardening charity, the Good Gardeners

Association, was another influential compost enthusiast, publishing his guide to *Compost Gardening* in 1972, as well as being a proselytizer of the no-dig method of organic cultivation (which views digging as detrimental to soil health).

Without chemical aids, the organic gardener relies not just on compost, but also on low-tech 'good practice'. Using techniques such as companion planting and crop rotation, and by maintaining good garden hygiene, selecting disease- and pest-resistant varieties, and encouraging beneficial predators into their plots – preferably those that eat slugs, snails and aphids – organic gardeners work with nature rather than against it.

Once considered eccentric and even contrarian, organic gardening has become mainstream, endorsed by high-profile gardeners (from royalty to award-winning chefs and TV pundits). Continuing concerns, too, over the safety of chemicals (those that have not been banned) keep organic gardening on the agenda.

GARDEN ROOMS

When laying out a **GARDEN FROM SCRATCH**, *gardeners face much the same challenge as writers when they contemplate a blank white page.* **A STRONG, COHERENT STRUCTURE** *is an essential starting point in both cases, and for the gardener,* **ORGANIZING SPACE INTO ROOMS** *can be an* **EFFECTIVE STRATEGY.**

❧

Dividing a garden into enclosed but connected spaces was a tenet of Arts and Crafts garden design, as recommended by the influential Edwardian landscape architect Thomas Mawson. In *The Art & Craft of Garden Making* (1900), he advised that gardens should be constructed around a 'series of apartments rather than a panorama which can be grasped in one view'. His book directly influenced the layout of gardens such as Lawrence Johnston's at Hidcote (started 1907), Cothay Manor in Somerset (laid out in the 1920s by Colonel Reggie Cooper) and Sissinghurst (created from the 1930s by Harold Nicolson and Vita Sackville-West) – all masterclasses in how the Arts and Crafts garden divided and conquered.

Creating a variety of spaces offers the gardener many advantages, not least the opportunity for theming. At Sissinghurst,

Harold Nicolson was the architect behind the garden's 'strictest formality of design', while Vita was in charge of planting, in which her aim was always 'the maximum informality'. Hidcote's 10 acres consist of over 20 garden rooms, including a holly avenue, a pool garden, a rose garden and the Pillar Garden. Cothay's numerous yew-hedged garden rooms lead off from a 180-metre (200-yard) walk, while Sissinghurst's rooms include a herb garden, a nuttery and Vita's famous White Garden. It is no coincidence that Johnston and VSW were passionate plants people; in the garden rooms and terraces at his Serre de la Madone garden in the south of France, Johnston was able to extend his planting repertoire to tropical and tender plants. In the somewhat less balmy climate of East Sussex, the garden rooms at Great Dixter offer a sheltered environment for tender plants, a service they also provide at Hidcote in the windswept and frost-prone Cotswolds.

The walls, hedges and fences that enclose garden rooms multiply the opportunities for flower-filled borders, strategically placed statuary, reflective ponds, or simply the soothing green caesura of a lawn (as in the Rondel, the circular garden within the Rose Garden at Sissinghurst). Vistas can be framed, and with one room linking to the next, tantalizing hints of what lies ahead can be glimpsed; garden rooms draw the eye and the visitor ever onward. Or, as Mawson put it, 'Art is well directed in arousing curiosity, always inviting further exploration'.

Garden rooms make large gardens feel more domestic and intimate in scale. Conversely, they make small gardens seem larger, and the monotony of a long, narrow town garden can be avoided by dividing the space into two or more rooms, using devices such as pergolas, patios, trellises or even a deeply undulating border.

HERBACEOUS BORDERS

Inspired by the artless charm of **COTTAGE GARDENS**, the herbaceous border was a **REBELLION** against formal, High Victorian gardens (which in turn had kicked against the pastoral landscapes of the previous century). It was a staple of the English **ARTS AND CRAFTS** garden and, in the hands of **GERTRUDE JEKYLL**, was raised to a fine art.

The herbaceous border was popularized by William Robinson in his 1883 book *The English Flower Garden*, naturalistic schemes using hardy herbaceous plants providing an antidote to what Robinson condemned as 'the false and hideous art' of carpet bedding. The double herbaceous border at Arley Hall in Cheshire is the oldest known example in England, and anticipated Robinson's approach by several decades, having been installed in 1851–52.

Humble country gardens may have been the source, but the herbaceous border in its pomp turned out to be anything but. Typically measuring around 60 metres long by 4 metres deep (200 by 14 feet), and usually set against the backdrop of a mellow stone or brick wall or an evergreen hedge, the herbaceous border was synonymous with the Edwardian country houses designed by Edwin Lutyens, and the gardens made for them by Gertrude Jekyll.

Conceived on a grand scale, herbaceous borders require a mastery of colour harmonies and plants to succeed – exactly the qualities that Jekyll, a painter and a skilled plantswoman, brought to her gardens. Jekyll's subtly orchestrated schemes included the border at her home at Munstead Wood, where the palette unfurled from cool to hot and back again along the length of the border. Plants

were arranged in drifts (Jekyll's word) of cool grey *Stachys* and *Santolina*, and fiery *Rudbeckia*, *Salvia*, *Kniphofia* and day lilies.

Jekyll's profoundly artistic approach to gardening continues to resonate. Her 1908 book *Colour Schemes for the Flower Garden* contained plans and pictures to help readers use plants to form 'beautiful pictures' and is still in print. Restorations of Jekyll's work can be seen at Upton Grey in Hampshire and at Hestercombe Gardens in Somerset, whose planting plans were discovered in a potting shed in 1973.

Designed to shine between May and September, the true herbaceous border dies down completely in winter, making it at odds with modern gardening's usual goal of year-round interest. It is labour-intensive, too, involving an assiduous regimen of staking, deadheading, plant division, weeding, mulching, feeding and tweaking. The magnificence of a herbaceous border in full flight, however, is hard to resist, and in 2016 Kew Gardens unveiled a new double herbaceous border along its Broad Walk. Extending some 320 metres (1,050 feet), and requiring 30,000 plants and a full-time staff of three, it is the longest herbaceous border in the world.

MIXED
BORDERS

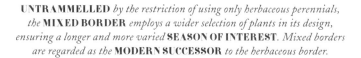

UNTRAMMELLED *by the restriction of using only herbaceous perennials,* the MIXED BORDER *employs a wider selection of plants in its design, ensuring a longer and more varied* SEASON OF INTEREST. *Mixed borders are regarded as the* MODERN SUCCESSOR *to the herbaceous border.*

Both the mixed and herbaceous border find their common ancestry in the influential writings of William Robinson, whose books *The Wild Garden* and *The English Flower Garden* were published in 1870 and 1883 respectively (the latter running to numerous editions well into the 1930s). Advocating a 'right plant in the right place' approach, Robinson practised what he preached by planting mixed perennial borders at his home, Gravetye Manor in Sussex, after his move there in 1884. Intensively planted for successive interest over an extended season, Robinson's borders continue to pay dividends now that Gravetye is run as a hotel with year-round visitors looking for year-round interest in its celebrated garden.

Incorporating bulbs, evergreens, trees, shrubs, climbers, roses, annuals and biennials, as well as hardy and tender perennials, the mixed border is a versatile and potentially flamboyant beast. The inclusion of tender plants and annuals allows schemes to be easily changed year on year, while exotics can add a real sense of drama. In recent years, the Red Borders at Hidcote have been updated with tropical bananas, cannas and lobelias, while the vibrant interplay of colours, textures and scale in the mixed borders at Great Dixter, the garden in East Sussex made famous by its doyen, the plantsman and writer Christopher Lloyd, have become that garden's signature. 'I see no point in segregating plants of differing habit or habits,' Lloyd wrote. 'They can all help each other.'

The inclusivity of the mixed border appeals to gardeners with plantaholic tendencies, as well as those with small gardens who cannot afford the dismal luxury of entire beds lying dormant all winter. The same principle applies to gardens that open to the public all year, such as at RHS Wisley, whose 128-metre (420-feet)-long double mixed borders are long enough to be able to accommodate a classically Jekyllian colour progression from pale pastels to hot reds and back again.

Abundance is a hallmark of the successful mixed border, and even before one plant has faded, its replacement has been plotted, placed and poised to perform; the mixed border is therefore hardly less labour-intensive than its herbaceous cousin. The mixed border is no place for half measures or bare earth, either, and nowhere is that generosity better demonstrated than at Sissinghurst, whose chatelaine Vita Sackville-West liked to 'cram, cram, cram every chink and cranny' of the garden with a cornucopia of plants.

ISLAND
BEDS

Popularized in the 1950s by the nurseryman
ALAN BLOOM, *island beds are made*
up of **HARDY PERENNIALS** *placed*
in the **MIDDLE OF A LAWN** *rather*
than in traditional rectilinear herbaceous
borders. Bloom maintained that these
perennials grew more robustly in such
FREESTANDING BEDS.

Considered an innovation when Bloom began planting them in his garden in Bressingham, Norfolk, in the mid-twentieth century, island beds were not a totally new idea. As early as 1771, such beds had been a feature of the flower garden designed by William Mason for the 2nd Earl Harcourt at Nuneham Courtenay; Victorians also deployed island beds in their formal gardens, setting them into lawns and using them as a vehicle for colourful displays of tender bedding plants.

Such was the hegemony of the long, deep Jekyll-style border in the first half of the twentieth century that Bloom's post-war island beds seemed radical. Growing hardy perennials in round or kidney-shaped beds replicated the exposed growing conditions of the nursery field, in which plants enjoyed good air flow and light throughout the day (as opposed to plants in a traditional border, where a wall, fence or hedge obstructed light for part of the day).

Convinced that plants grew more sturdily this way, with less need for laborious staking and cosseting, Bloom popularized the concept in books such as *Perennials in Island Beds* (1977) and created some 48 island beds in the Dell Garden at Bressingham; both although they still depended on having a nicely kept lawn to act as a foil, island beds became hugely popular.

From 1967, Alan's son Adrian Bloom developed the concept of conifer beds in his adjacent Foggy Bottom garden; these island beds were planted with evergreen conifers and underplanted with heathers and other ericaceous plants for year-round interest and colour. Conifer beds rapidly became part

were an effective showcase for the style, and for the perennials he grew and sold at his nursery (among whose notable introductions were *Crocosmia* 'Lucifer' and *Achillea* 'Moonshine'). Displayed in island beds, plants could be enjoyed, like so many theatrical productions of the day, 'in the round', and unlike herbaceous borders, did not necessarily require a big garden to accommodate them; of the gardening zeitgeist of the 60s and 70s, although the style subsequently fell sharply from favour as the conifers inevitably outgrew their welcome. However, new dwarf varieties of coniferous plants, such as *Pinus mugo* 'Mops', may yet result in a comeback of the conifer island bed – worse aspects of the 1970s having inexplicably already enjoyed revivals.

ALLOTMENTS

When the going gets tough, the **TOUGH GET GROWING** *:*
cultivating food for personal consumption has always been one
of the **MAIN MOTIVATIONS** *behind having an* **ALLOTMENT.**
Vegetable plots for **GARDENLESS GARDENERS** *became*
commonplace as urbanization increased during the nineteenth
century, and fulfilled an important role in **FOOD PRODUCTION**
during the two world wars.

During the heyday of the British allotment movement during the interwar period, over 1.5 million allotments were 'Dug for Victory' when shipping blockades disrupted food imports and rationing was imposed. Enthusiasm for cultivating a patch of rented land the size of a tennis court waned in the UK after World War II, but has increased sharply recently, following food-security scandals and environmental concerns. According to the National Allotment Society, there are currently some 330,000 allotment plots in the UK, with around 100,000 people waiting to get their hands on one.

Intended for people with no access to a garden of their own, allotments began as a piecemeal, usually charitable, response to land Enclosure Acts that deprived the rural poor of access to common land from the seventeenth century onwards. The Industrial Revolution and mass migration of rural workers to towns and cities, and the crippling

poverty endured by the working classes, galvanized the allotment movement in the nineteenth century, and in 1887 the Allotments Act required local authorities to provide allotments if there were demand.

Successive acts of parliament shaped the British allotment through the twentieth century, from the Small Holdings and Allotments Act of 1908 and continuing up to the Allotment Act of 1950 (which permitted the keeping of hens and rabbits). Some aspects of allotment administration remain resolutely archaic, such as the practice of measuring plots in poles, rods or perches, a pole being an Anglo-Saxon unit of measurement equivalent to 5½ yards (5 metres). A standard UK allotment is usually 10 poles, or 250 square metres. Tenancy quit notices still expire on the traditional quarter days of Lady Day (in March) and Michaelmas (in September).

Not all allotments were purely utilitarian veg plots. Detached town gardens were a type of allotment that developed in Britain in the mid-nineteenth century that were as much about recreation and quality family time as they were about putting food on the table. The recently restored Hill Close Gardens in Warwick are a good example of the genre, with neatly trimmed hedge boundaries enclosing lawns and areas where tenants could raise fruit and vegetables, and pigs and poultry. To make the most of their outside amenity, tenants of such 'guinea gardens' (city centre-based skilled workers and artisans who could afford the comparatively high rents) built little brick summerhouses in which they could shelter from the weather, cook a meal or relax.

In Germany, similar gardens were inspired by the teachings of Dr Daniel Schreber, a naturopath who advocated outdoor pursuits such as gardening as a healthy pastime for young people (diverting them from teenage pursuits such as masturbation). The first Schrebergarten was established in Leipzig in 1864, and the concept of the recreational yet productive garden 'colony' quickly spread across northern Europe. Today there are over a million such kleingartens in Germany, each plot typically measuring 200–400 square metres (2,150–4,300 square feet) and with a summerhouse, customized according to its owner's taste and budget. Kleingartens are strictly regulated both at federal and at site level, where rules might specify what crops can be grown, the height of hedging, and how often to mow and weed.

Despite the brevity of their summers, Scandinavian countries also embraced the Schrebergarten ideal, and in the Swedish kolonilotter, the garden shed has become the urban equivalent of the stuga or country cottages where many Swedes spend the summer months. The world's most northerly allotments are in Rovaniemi, Finland (better known as the official home of Santa Claus, so now we can make an educated guess as to how he keeps busy in the summer).

Beacons of independence and self-expression, allotments have evolved into a distinct garden type in which good taste is beside the point and where the make-do-and-mend ethos still thrives. Allotments are gardens for the everyman, a place where even the most dyed-in-the-wool urbanite can connect with their inner peasant and enjoy the simple satisfactions of growing food and flowers.

POTAGERS

Derived from the French **WORD FOR SOUP**
*(potage), the potager is, by extension, the place
where the ingredients for said soup are grown – in*
PLAIN ENGLISH, *the* **'KITCHEN GARDEN'.**

The *potager décoratif* is a productive garden in its Sunday best, with fruit, vegetables, flowers and herbs arranged as much for their aesthetic effect as for their yield. In these formally laid-out gardens, the humble vegetable is elevated to ornamental status.

Although the potager's origins are monastic, it was Renaissance gardeners, with their love of pattern, geometry and sense of occasion, who transformed the humble veg patch into showpiece gardens, where visitors could stroll and admire the latest novelties from the New World.

At Versailles, the potager laid out for King Louis XIV by Jean-Baptiste de la Quintinie between 1678 and 1683 was the gold standard of *potagers décoratifs*. Extending to over 23 acres and arranged around a central fountain in a formation of squares (the best shape for a potager, in La Quintinie's opinion), the Potager du Roi was a favourite haunt of the French king, who learned how to train fruit trees there. La Quintinie, who went on to write the era's standard work on productive gardening (*Instructions pour les Jardins Fruitiers et Potagers*, 1690) ran the Potager du Roi on adventurous lines, using new ideas such as hot beds and glass cloches in order to produce vegetables out of season for the royal household. After the Revolution, the potager became a horticultural school, and present-day students still cultivate a hefty tonnage of fruit and veg there each year.

While Versailles is a unique survivor, the potager at the Château de Villandry in the Loire is an early twentieth-century recreation of a Renaissance parterre garden. Conceived, like Versailles, on a grand scale, its dazzlingly geometric box-edged beds contain ramrod rows of colour-coordinated vegetables, which are treated as bedding plants, with twice-yearly planting changes.

In the 1980s, Rosemary Verey, a grande dame of British gardening, was likewise inspired by historic precedent to revive the potager on a more domestic scale. The potager she made at her Cotswolds home was highly influential, with its tunnel of trained fruit trees, topiary and box hedges, and colourful vegetables interplanted with fragrant rosemary and lavender. Mainstream interest was further piqued by two programmes aired on BBC TV in the late 1980s – *The Victorian Kitchen Garden* and *The Ornamental Kitchen Garden*.

In the 1990s, after decades of decline, and even dereliction, the walled kitchen gardens of English country houses became a focus for restoration, often with volunteers taking the place of the trained gardeners who once toiled in them. In 1995, Beningbrough Hall in Yorkshire became one of the first of 30 such gardens to be restored by the National Trust, who then launched an appeal in 2014 to raise funds to restore the remaining 110 walled gardens in their care.

CONTAINER GARDENING

The beauty of container gardening lies in its **FLEXIBILITY** *and* **PORTABILITY**. *Plants in pots can make a garden where the soil is poor, or space at a* **PREMIUM**. *Even in capacious gardens, strategically placed container plants can add a welcome splash of seasonal colour to flower beds in need of some* **EXTRA OOMPH**.

Perhaps the most stylish containers are the ones designed in the seventeenth century by André Le Nôtre for the citrus trees at Versailles. King Louis XIV's enormous collection of citrus and other tender trees was overwintered in the orangery there – a transhumance that took place every November and April and required portability on a grand scale. Painted in the palace's signature shade of green, the square planters (*caisses à oranger*) were made from oak and cast iron, with pine cone finials, and in a variety of sizes to accommodate trees of all ages. Each of the four sides could be hinged out or detached to allow for root pruning, soil replenishment, and to remove the plant if it needed potting on. In Le Nôtre's day, a horse-drawn contraption moved the trees in their planters, a job today performed by tractor and trailer.

For those on a less-than-imperial budget (modern Versailles planters cost a princely packet), terracotta plant pots are an attractive option. Ornamental terracotta pots were a feature of Renaissance Italian gardens (and often as not planted with citrus trees), but simple earthenware pots were the workhorses of the nursery trade and everyday gardening. These were manufactured in industrial quantities in the nineteenth century, by companies such as Sankey of Bulwell, Nottinghamshire. Founded in 1855, Sankey was capable of turning out 60,000 handmade pots and saucers in a day, but by the mid-1960s the majority of their pots were made of injection-moulded plastic – lighter and less breakable than earthenware, and a boon for the fledgling garden centre trade.

Particular plants required specialized pots. 'Long Toms' were for bulbs, shallow 'pans' were for alpines, while orchid pots had drainage holes at the sides to encourage roots. A favourite of eighteenth-century 'florists', auriculas were traditionally grown in terracotta pots and displayed in 'theatres', a seasonal container garden that could be easily squeezed into a cramped city courtyard.

Window boxes were another egalitarian form of container gardening in the eighteenth and nineteenth centuries, made possible in part by the advent of sash windows. Books advised what plants to use, and how to care for them. Virginia creeper was recommended for window gardening by Thomas Fairchild in his 1722 book *The City Gardener*, while Elizabeth Kent's 1823 guide *Flora Domestica, or The Portable Flower Garden*, recognizing that potted plants were at the mercy of inexperienced gardeners, offered full 'directions for the treatment of plants in pots'. Container gardening is pursued no less enthusiastically in the twenty-first century, its most colourful incarnations being the hanging baskets, troughs and plants of civic schemes.

TAXONOMY AND NOMENCLATURE

*Although the word '*TAXONOMY*' (meaning the science of classification) was first coined in the nineteenth century, mankind has been trying to* CATEGORIZE *the natural world since antiquity.* ARISTOTLE *came up with a* RUDIMENTARY *system that separated the animal and plant kingdoms, and his pupil Theophrastus (*'THE FATHER OF BOTANY'*) identified around 500 named plants, dividing them into trees, shrubs, sub-shrubs and herbs.*

In the seventeenth century, John Ray developed a taxonomic system using the physical characteristics of plants as a way of determining their relationships to each other and dividing them for the first time into monocots and dicots. Ray's *Historia Plantarum*, published in three volumes between 1686 and 1704, is regarded as the first textbook of modern botany and earned him the title of 'the English Linnaeus'.

By the eighteenth century, the huge influx of newly discovered plants to the Western world was making life tricky for botanists – not least in the matter of knowing what to call them all. Latin, the universal language of learning, imposed some discipline, but with no international standard, plants acquired numerous synonyms. To add to the confusion, names included lengthy descriptions of defining characteristics, saddling even a commonplace plant like the briar rose with the cumbersome title of *Rosa sylvestris alba cum rubore, folio glabro*. Common names offered no more clarity, being specific to particular countries or even regions.

It was left to the actual, Swedish, Linnaeus to rationalize scientific nomenclature in the eighteenth century. Linnaeus's masterstroke was realizing that plants did not need to be described, but could be simply designated using just two Latin words to denote a plant's genus, and its unique species. Thus the briar rose became the easy-to-remember, perfectly distinguishable *Rosa canina*.

As professor of botany at Uppsala University, Linnaeus made taxonomy his life's work, dispatching his students (known as 'apostles') to procure specimens from around the world, and promoting his ideas in books, such as his 1753 *Species Plantarum*, in which he named and categorized some 1,000 genera and 6,000 plant species. No wonder he felt able to boast, with characteristic immodesty, 'God created, but Linnaeus organized'.

Over two centuries after his death in 1778, Linnaeus is still organizing. His binomial system became the international scientific standard for naming plants and animals, and many of his original names live on, too, his *Species Plantarum* having been designated the earliest acceptable source by the International Code of Botanical Nomenclature.

Linnaeus's method of classifying plants according to the number and arrangement of their sexual parts proved less enduring. Condemned as 'loathsome harlotry' and disliked for its artificiality in some quarters, Linnaean taxonomy gained some currency, but within a century had been superseded by 'natural' systems, such as those devised by Antoine-Laurent de Jussieu in France, and by George Bentham and Joseph Dalton Hooker in Britain, which took into account a range of plant characteristics.

The arrival of DNA sequencing in the 1990s upset the taxonomic apple cart, revealing evolutionary relationships between plants previously thought to be unrelated.

A new, molecular-based classification system, the Angiosperm Phylogeny Group (APG I), was launched in 1998; the latest revision, APG IV, was published in 2016. Thanks to the group's findings, whole plant orders have been deleted, new ones created and an array of garden stalwarts reassigned to different genera – and renamed accordingly. Grudgingly, gardeners now have to remember that Michaelmas daisies, known from Linnaean times as asters, must now be referred to as *Symphyotrichum*, that *Senecio* now goes by *Brachyglottis*, and that *Schizostylis* are actually *Hesperantha*. Perhaps there's something to be said for common names after all.

BOTANIC GARDENS

Botanic gardens **EVOLVED** *from monastic physic gardens and were originally places where* **MEDICINAL PLANTS** *were grown and studied. The world's first* ⬝⬝⬝ ⬝⬝⬝ ⬝⬝⬝⬝⬝ ⬝⬝⬝⬝⬝⬝ ⬝⬝⬝⬝⬝⬝ ⬝⬝⬝⬝⬝⬝⬝⬝ ⬝⬝⬝⬝ ⬝⬝⬝ ⬝⬝⬝⬝⬝⬝ ⬝ ⬝⬝⬝⬝⬝ ⬝⬝ ⬝⬝⬝ ⬝,⬝⬝⬝.

Where Renaissance Italy led, Europe followed, with physic gardens being established at universities around the continent. The botanic garden at Leiden University was set up in 1590, and had the good fortune of having the Flemish botanist Carolus Clusius as its first director. Having previously run the imperial botanic garden in Vienna, Clusius had an enviable international address book, and his introductions to Holland included tulips from the East and exotic New World novelties such as tobacco and tomatoes.

Universities did not have a monopoly on botanic gardens: the sixteenth-century surgeon-botanist John Gerard cultivated his own *hortus medicus* in Clerkenwell, while the Jardin des Plantes in Paris originated as King Louis XIII's personal medicinal garden, the Jardin du Roi. Kew Gardens was developed with botanic intent first by Princess Augustus from 1759, and later under Sir Joseph Banks, who envisioned it as 'a great botanical exchange house for the empire'.

Centres of knowledge in an expanding world, botanic gardens amassed plants sent by explorers and mercantile enterprises such as the East India Company. Empire-building countries set up satellite gardens where lucrative crops like tea, coffee and rubber could be established or acclimatized. In 1793, Britain's first colonial botanic garden, on St Vincent, was the destination for Captain Bligh's ill-starred breadfruit plants, while in 1832 the botanic garden in Sydney helped found the Australian wine industry, when it received a collection of vines from botanic gardens in Europe.

The exchange of economically valuable plants and seeds could backfire. France was able to establish a thriving coffee industry on Martinique in the 1720s on the strength of some

coffee plants given to the Jardin du Roi by the botanic garden in Amsterdam.

As botany became a subject in its own right, botanic gardens arranged their plants in 'order beds' where scientists could study plant classification. Taxonomy being a developing subject, botanic gardens periodically rearrange their order beds according to the prevailing system (not always to the delight of their gardeners). At Kew the order beds follow the latest Angiosperm Phylogeny Group system, replacing a previous layout that reflected the nineteenth-century Bentham and Hooker system, which in turn replaced a layout following Antoine-Laurent de Jussieu's 'natural' system.

The practice of drying plant specimens was pioneered at Padua and Bologna in the sixteenth century. Over the years, these diligently assembled 'dry gardens' have

developed into extensive herbariums (the one at Kew runs to some 7 million specimens). Correctly dried plants can last indefinitely, meaning that historic specimens collected by Sir Hans Sloane, Charles Darwin and William Hooker in the eighteenth and nineteenth centuries can still be referenced today.

Where once botanic gardens majored in exploitation, today's emphasis is on conservation, and providing a safe haven for plants endangered by climate change and other environmental challenges. With one in five plant species facing extinction globally, seed banks at botanic gardens around the world, such as Kew's Millennium Seed Bank, provide the final backup by saving seeds for a rainy – or a very dry – day.

HORTUS CONCLUSUS

From Roman courtyards to contemporary pocket parks, the aesthetic and practical appeal of an **ENCLOSED GARDEN** *is enduring.* **GOOD FENCES** *not only make for* **GOOD NEIGHBOURS**, *they also keep interlopers (animal and human) at bay,* **ENSURE PRIVACY** *and provide an attractive backdrop for plants.*

The medieval garden was born out of all these considerations; built within the curtilage of manor house, monastery or castle, the *hortus conclusus* (enclosed garden) was the prototypical 'garden room' – an inward-looking garden that offered at least the illusion of a safe haven in a bellicose age.

Medieval manuscript illuminations and devotional images suggest what such gardens might have looked like: flower-studded lawns, turf benches, rose-woven trellises, shady arbours and playing fountains are recurring features within their boundary walls.

The enclosed garden was also a feminine space; rich in allegory, it was associated with the Virgin but resonant of sexier Old Testament gardens – the lost paradise of Eden, and the Song of Songs ('a garden enclosed is my sister, my spouse; a spring shut up; a fountain sealed').

Although the *hortus conclusus* of Marian imagery was devoutly chaste, its secular equivalent was a garden of earthly delight, a pleasant place (the *locus amoenus* of classical literature) where the rituals of courtly love could be played out. In the thirteenth-century tale of courtly love *Roman de la Rose*, the character of the Lover quests for his Rose, and finds her in a walled garden owned by a nobleman called Pleasure.

Sequestered monastic gardens, where monks grew fruit, vegetables and healing herbs, blended the practical with the pious. Manual labour such as gardening was central to the Rule of St Benedict, and the individual cells of solitary Carthusian monks even came with their own en-suite gardens.

The ideal monastery layout, as depicted in the ninth-century 'St Gall plan', envisaged several enclosed gardens, including an orchard (which doubled up as the monks' cemetery), a physic garden, and two 'paradise gardens' at either end of the church, where flowers for the church would have been grown. At the heart of any monastery – ideal or otherwise – lay the most enclosed garden of all, the cloister garth, a contemplative space whose green lawn and central fountain provided spiritual refreshment.

Most modern urban and suburban gardens are *horti conclusi* – whether demarcated by wooden fence or leylandii hedge, they are sanctuaries from the outside world, a place to play, potter, entertain friends, and perhaps even pursue a romance.

ENGLISH LANDSCAPE
GARDENS

⊃∞∞⊂

English garden designers in the **EIGHTEENTH CENTURY** *took their inspiration from Italy's classical and* **RENAISSANCE** *past to create gardens that evoked the idealized landscapes painted by* **NICOLAS POUSSIN** *and* **CLAUDE LORRAIN**.

The landscape garden was the dominant garden style of the long Georgian century that began when George I ascended the British throne in 1714. The overbearing Baroque style associated with the absolutism of French monarchs was replaced by the pared-down Palladian architecture promoted by Lord Burlington, and naturalistic gardens that 'called in' the countryside beyond.

Horace Walpole credited Burlington's protégé William Kent as the man who first 'leapt the fence and saw all nature as a garden'. A multitalented painter, architect and designer who was well versed in the classical idiom, having spent ten years working in Rome, Kent helped his patrons implement the fashionable new style when he returned to England in 1719, working at Chiswick House, Claremont and Stowe, and softening the formality of their existing gardens.

Rousham Park, laid out in the 1730s, shows Kent's willingness to 'consult the genius of the place', as recommended by the poet and commentator Alexander Pope. Here Kent conjured an Arcadian landscape by the banks of the River Cherwell, using a ha-ha

to blend the surrounding parkland into the lawns near the house, adding distant eye catchers, and designing a sequence of gloomy glades and sunlit lawns enlivened by temples, cascades, terraces and statues. Conceived as an emotional, even theatrical experience, the garden has to be walked through following a particular route to appreciate its full impact.

If Kent was the founding father of early landscape gardening, Lancelot 'Capability' Brown was the master of its mature style. Brown, who honed his skills working under William Kent at Stowe in the 1740s, became the most prolific and sought-after landscaper of his day, thanks to his gift for exploiting the 'capabilities' of estates, and ability to delegate jobs to trusted on-site workers.

Brown's rolling parklands, enclosed by wooded shelter belts and choreographed with clumps of specimen trees, winding carriage drives and huge naturalistic lakes spanned by statement bridges, became synonymous with the English landscape style. Some 150 of them survive to this day.

Often working on a vast scale, Brown could be uncompromising. At Blenheim

Palace, where he was occupied for over a decade, he dammed the River Glyme to create a suitably scaled 40-acre lake for the huge estate. At Petworth House, where he worked in the 1750s and 60s, Brown rerouted a main road and overwrote the existing formal garden to bring the parkland right up to the house. The landscape at Milton Abbey required the removal of an entire village (although Brown did design a model village, Milton Abbas, by way of alternative lodgings for its inhabitants).

Eye-wateringly expensive to install – Brown's contracts at Petworth would be worth about £9 million in today's money – once in place, landscape gardens were cheaper to run than formal gardens and, with their extensive pastures and woodland, more productive.

After Brown's death in 1783, Humphry Repton became England's leading landscaper, working in Brownian vein but reintroducing formal elements such as terraces and flower gardens near the house. The first person to describe himself as a 'landscape gardener', Repton was also a competent watercolourist who used this skill to good effect in his 'Red Books', devising ingenious overlays to show prospective clients 'before' and 'after' views of their properties.

Despite Pope's dictum that 'all gardening is landscape painting', eighteenth-century gardens were not simply to be looked at, they were spaces to be experienced, where people could stroll, picnic, bathe and go boating. With their Elysian Fields and Temples of Apollo, gardens expressed the cultural values and sometimes – as in the monuments devised by Lord Cobham at Stowe – even the political views of their owners. The garden created at Painshill Park by the Hon. Charles Hamilton, on the other hand, had no such subtext. Its parade of follies – everything from a Turkish tent to a crystal grotto and Gothic tower – were intended only to surprise and delight and, recently restored, still do.

WILDERNESS GARDENS

A **FASHIONABLE** *feature of mid-seventeenth and early eighteenth-century gardens, 'wildernesses' were anything but wild.* **ESSENTIALLY** **FORMAL**, *wildernesses were a kind of* **SECLUDED** *woodland parterre, set at a distance from the house, and divided by straight hedge-lined allées, radiating out from a central focal point.*

Italian Renaissance gardens inspired the first wildernesses in the UK – Lord Lumley's garden at Nonsuch Palace, created in the 1580s following a visit to Italy, featured a wilderness, while a *bosco* (little wood) was one of several Italianate touches in the gardens laid out by Lord Burghley at Theobalds between 1575 and 1585.

Wildernesses were a presence in Baroque gardens; the formal gardens designed by Isaac de Caus at Wilton House in the 1630s included twin wildernesses, placed like a woodland buffer zone between the parterre and plat gardens, and bisected by the garden's broad main axis. Statues of Flora and Bacchus, appropriately rustic classical deities, presided over a clearing at the heart of each wilderness.

By 1735 wildernesses were so ubiquitous that Philip Miller, gardener at the Chelsea Physic Garden, could describe 'the usual method' of making them in his *Gardner's Dictionary* as a process that involved dividing the terrain 'into squares, angles, circles or other figures ... the walks are commonly made to intersect each other in angles'.

Most wildernesses were destroyed or altered by the landscape revolution instigated by the capable Mr Brown and his successors. Some, such as at Chatsworth House and Clandon Park House, were recorded for posterity by Leonard Knyff and Jan Kip, whose bird's-eye perspectives of English country estates were published in the early eighteenth century.

Knyff's c. 1702–14 painting of Hampton Court Palace shows the wilderness installed for William III by fashionable garden designers London and Wise, the vestige of which survives as the maze. As this implies, wildernesses, with their hedges and criss-crossing paths, were places for getting enjoyably lost in, as well as for enjoying nature. The glades in the restored seventeenth-century wilderness at Ham House are furnished with rustic kiosks, ideal for reading or a private conversation. At Versailles, the woodland *bosquets* designed by André Le Nôtre between 1663 and 1685 were altogether more stagey; hidden behind trellises and liberally furnished with waterworks and statuary, they were used for royal entertainments, as well as discreet rendezvous.

The English wilderness was more low key. John Evelyn, the seventeenth-century gardening authority, advocated 'confused and irregular planting', interplanting the trees with 'thickets'

of hazel, birch and hawthorn, in turn underplanting these with shade-loving flowers such as periwinkle. This 'height-order' approach can still be seen at St Paul's Walden Bury, whose early eighteenth-century wilderness consists of three grassy rides radiating from a *patte d'oie* (goose foot) opening. The hedges that define the rides are kept low, and the shrubs behind them coppiced, so that the taller 'plumes' of lime, chestnut and oak trees behind them are seen to best advantage.

From around 1710, irregular serpentine paths began to replace the regimented symmetry of the early wildernesses. Later in the century, woodland areas became a focus for plantations of the new American trees and shrubs being sent over to England by plant hunters such as John Bartram. Gradually the closed-in wilderness opened up and evolved into that quintessentially nineteenth-century feature, the shrubbery.

PRAIRIE
PLANTING

❦

Also known as the **DUTCH WAVE**
or the **NEW PERENNIAL** *movement, this
planting style features large,* **NATURALISTIC**
*drifts of perennials and grasses, often using plants of
North American origin. Fashionable since the late
1990s, prairie planting can be seen in* **ALL THE
RIGHT GARDENS** *on both sides of the pond.*

❧

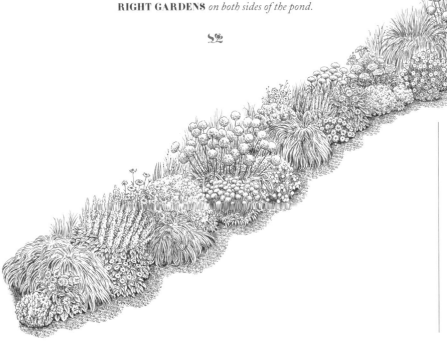

The style developed not on the American plains but in the nurseries of northern Europe, where Dutch and German horticulturalists such as Karl Foerster (1874–1970) and his protégé Ernst Pagels (1913–2007) had been breeding new cultivars of hardy perennials such as the feather reed grass *Calamagrostis x acutiflora* 'Karl Foerster', and *Miscanthus sinensis* 'Kleine Fontäne'.

At his garden and nursery near Potsdam, Foerster used his plants in experimental naturalistic schemes, but it is the Dutch landscape designer and erstwhile nurseryman Piet Oudolf (b. 1944) who has put these gardenworthy new perennials on the international garden map in the twenty-first century, with high-profile projects such as the regeneration of the High Line in New York.

Initially influenced by the formalism of Dutch landscape architect Mien Ruys (whose own nursery introduced the prairie-planting staple *Helenium* 'Moerheim Beauty' in 1930), Oudolf has evolved his own style, massing swathes of perennials and grasses in nuanced, naturalistic combinations. His schemes appear in English country settings such as RHS Wisley (2001) and the Walled Garden at Scampston in North Yorkshire (opened to the public in 2005), as well as ultra-urban sites such as Chicago's Lurie Garden, whose 'perennial meadows' showcase many native American prairie species (the result of Oudolf's research trips to the prairies of the Midwest to see plants growing in the wild).

The New Perennial aesthetic embraces seasonal decline, with plants being allowed to stand, seed heads intact, through autumn and winter. Plants are selected for longevity and as much for their architectural form and ability to die elegantly as for their colour, the idea being that desiccated stems and seed heads in shades of brown look sensational in frost and snow (but less so, critics of the movement argue, in warm, wet winters).

Signature 'prairie' plants include North American natives such as *Rudbeckia*, *Helenium*, *Echinacea*, *Penstemon* and *Eupatorium*, whose ability to associate well visually, and live long and prosper through cold winters and dry summers also appeals to ecologically minded New Perennialists. With summer deadheading off the agenda, perennial schemes instead require an annual late winter mow (herds of bison need not apply).

Despite appearances, prairie planting is anything but naturalistic. Skilfully selected cultivars arranged in painstakingly planned combinations ensure that this style, as Oudolf puts it, 'reminds you of nature even though it isn't'. And for all its supposed novelty, the New Perennial movement shares a common ancestor in William Robinson's 'wild gardening' approach, while also obeying the conventional gardening wisdom of the right plant in the right place.

ZEN GARDENS

*Japanese gardens make most Western gardens look positively
SLAPDASH in comparison. Every ELEMENT
is carefully considered, with little left to CHANCE.*

This is an approach that has been followed for centuries, as Japan's oldest gardening book makes clear. Written in the eleventh century by a courtier, the *Sakuteiki* ('Records of Garden Making') advised on allegorical meaning as well as design and maintenance, including matters such as the proper placement of ⟨⟨⟨⟨⟨ (with dire warnings of what ⟨⟨⟨ would become of those who violated the stringent rules). The author also instructed on timeless basic principles, such as choosing a suitable site, as well as the technicalities of digging water features and creating islands.

A reverence for nature and a profound spirituality has been embedded in Japanese gardens for centuries; Shinto, Taoism and Buddhism each played a part in shaping them. Zen Buddhism gave rise to Japan's most iconic garden type, the *kare-sansui* (dry landscape) temple gardens that were developed in the medieval period. Contained within a walled enclosure, these ascetic monastic gardens are static entities, designed to be contemplated from an elevated platform ⟨⟨⟨⟨⟨⟨⟨⟨⟨⟨⟨⟨⟨⟨ and any wider landscape visible beyond the walls, they are devoid of living plants and consist instead of groups of stones set into a sea of sand or gravel, which is raked by monks into furrowed patterns to denote ripples or waves.

Within the dry landscape, carefully selected and grouped stones evoke features such as mountains or islands. Stones were

50

so central to the concept of what constituted a garden that garden landscapers were known as *ishi-tate-so*, or 'monks who arrange stones'. At Ryoan-ji, the fifteenth-century Temple of the Peaceful Dragon in Kyoto, the garden's 15 stones can never be seen all at the same time, and are variously said to represent a tigress guiding her cubs across a pond, the outline of a branch, mountains, or a group of islands. All is indeed illusion in a Zen garden.

In contrast to enclosed temple gardens, the secular stroll gardens, or *kaiyushiki-teien*, created from the seventeenth century by samurai lords, were outward-facing and designed to be walked through. Developed at a time when travel outside Japan was banned, these 'excursion gardens' led walkers on a tour of popular Japanese and Chinese landscapes, whose mountains, lakes, waterfalls and bridges were recreated in miniaturized form (*shukkei*).

At the Koishikawa Korakuen Gardens in Tokyo, begun in 1629 by the Mito Tokogawa family, the itinerary recreated the sights of the Nakasendo trade route, centring on a scaled-down rendition of Lake Biwa. The garden's original 65 acres were themselves miniaturized down to 16.5 acres by Tokyo's urbanization in the modern era. Winding pathways enhanced the garden's sense of space, as did the carefully framed views of the wider landscape beyond, using the technique of *shakkei*, or 'borrowed scenery'.

WHITE GARDENS

PALE IS INTERESTING *when it comes to white gardens.* The ULTIMATE EXERCISE IN RESTRAINT, *white garden 'rooms' are particularly associated with the* ARTS AND CRAFTS STYLE *of gardening.*

The most famous White Garden of them all is that made by Vita Sackville-West at Sissinghurst in 1949/50, Vita having shared her plans for 'my grey, green and white garden' with her *Observer* readers in January 1949.

Vita's new white garden replaced a rose garden, but roses were still present (how could they not be at Sissinghurst?); at the garden's centre was a *Rosa mulliganii*, while assorted white roses rambled through an avenue of white-blossom-bearing almond trees. Designed to be savoured as much by night as by day, the garden was planted with a moonglow palette of white flowering plants: gladioli, 'White Pearl' irises, delphiniums, *Campanula*, *Gypsophila*, white peonies and hydrangeas, set off by grey foliage plants such as *Santolina*, *Cineraria* and *Artemisia*, and contained within beds edged with dark green box.

White (sometimes known as 'ghost' gardens) were not a new idea when Vita implemented her scheme at Sissinghurst; they had been fashionable on both sides of the Atlantic between the wars, and were a feature of Arts and Crafts gardens, such as Hidcote, and at Barrington Court, whose White Garden Gertrude Jekyll helped design in 1917.

Jekyll, the doyenne of horticultural colour coordination, was a discerning advocate of restricted colour schemes, devoting a chapter to 'Gardens of Special Colouring' in her influential 1908 book *Colour Schemes for the Flower Border*. In this she proposed a grey garden as one of a sequence of blue, orange, gold and green gardens (the grey sitting between the orange and gold). In her own garden at Munstead Wood, lack of space meant Jekyll had to be satisfied with a short length of double border for her 'little grey garden'. Designed to look at its best in August, this cool scheme of white, pink and

shades of purple was underpinned by grey foliage plants such as catmint and lavender.

For Jekyll, 'special colouring' did not mean the slavish pursuit of a single colour; she was dismissive of those who talked of gardens filled exclusively with blue or white plants. In Jekyll's hands, a grey garden was not a grisly grisaille, but a subtly calibrated composition, in which the colours and tones of carefully selected plants such as Ceanothus 'Gloire de Versailles' and Clematis 'Jackmanii' were deemed to be 'just right'. White can be right, but it must also be beautiful.

THE
ANTI-LAWN

While books furnish a room, nothing quite sets off a garden like a lawn – even **MEDIEVAL MONKS** *liked them, believing the colour green to be refreshing to the soul – and since the invention of the lawnmower, a patch of emerald greensward has become an essential in even the smallest garden. Few things equal the* **SENSUOUS PLEASURE** *of walking barefoot on closely shorn grass, either. But has the quintessential English lawn become too successful, having been exported to climates that are* **UNSUITED TO ITS DEMANDS** *?*

Turf grass needs water, a commodity usually in lamentably ready supply during the average northern-hemisphere summer but less so, say, during the recent four-year Californian drought. Watering is one of the chores attendant on a luscious lawn, along with the chemical weeding, feeding and pest control usually deemed necessary for grassy perfection. America's estimated 30 million acres of lawns use ten times more chemical pesticides per acre than agricultural land, and it has been mooted that turf grass is the US's biggest irrigated 'crop', soaking up 270 billion gallons of water weekly.

Monastic lawns may offer spiritual balm, but for the gardener the tyranny of the weekly mow and the seasonal round of scarification, aeration, sanding, reseeding and rolling can be less than edifying. The ecological toll of lawncare, too, has prompted a backlash. The doyenne of the natural landscaping movement in America, Lorrie Otto, blasted lawns as 'sheared, poisoned, monotonous, sterile landscapes' and advocated using native plants in their place. Her vision continues in the Wild Ones, a not-for-profit that has dedicated itself to 'healing the Earth, one yard at a time' since 1979.

Founded in 1997, Smaller American Lawns Today (SALT) also promotes native plants and suggests managing lawns as meadows as part of its mission to create 'more harmonious, productive, ecologically sound and naturalistic landscapes'. And in a sign that the anti-lawn might be going mainstream, the US Environmental Protection Agency now advises homeowners to use 'regionally appropriate' plants to create a 'water smart' landscape.

Another 1990s idea, the Freedom Lawn, is less prescriptive; its laissez-faire approach avoids irrigation and regular mowing, and encourages plants that would be usually classed as lawn weeds (clover, plantains, dandelions and chickweed) to self-seed among the grass. Another solution is to turn lawns into vegetable gardens, such as the first Edible Estate created by artist Fritz Haeg in Salina, Kansas, in 2005, and later in such locations across the globe as Rome, Istanbul and Budapest. The most radical alternative – artificial grass – is also gaining popularity as an environmentally friendly lawn alternative, although it is regarded in some quarters as the horticultural equivalent of vegetarian sausages.

WATER FEATURES

Water is a great medium for SHOWING OFF –
just look at the huge canal in front of the TAJ MAHAL,
the self-mythologizing fountains commissioned by
Louis XIV at VERSAILLES, *or the irrepressible*
GIOCHI D'AQUA *at the Villa d'Este.*

Practical or playful, water has been a component of garden design since classical times, from the symbolic 'four rivers' of the Persian *chahar bagh* to the virtuoso hydraulics of Renaissance and Baroque gardens. As always, size matters. The cascade built by the 1st Duke of Devonshire at Chatsworth House in the early eighteenth century descends 60 metres (200 feet) over a series of steps, each group of which is different, so the water changes sound as it rushes downhill. It is still impressive and in 2004 was voted the UK's best water feature by *Country Life* magazine. Chatsworth's watery one-upmanship continued in the nineteenth century with the Emperor Fountain, whose record breaking 90-metre (290-feet)-high jet was designed to outdo the Russian tsar's fountain at Peterhof (and did).

These days, even the smallest back yard is likely to boast a water feature of some description, an electric pump endlessly circulating

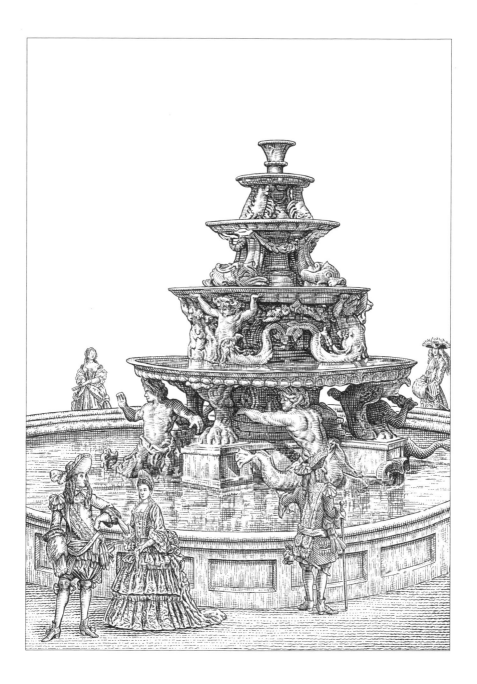

a few litres of water between feature and reservoir. Lowly or grand, water features can trace their ancestry back to ancient forebears: the cooling canals and rills of Persian paradise gardens, the noisy *chadar* water screens of Kashmiri gardens, the fountains and basins of Roman peristyle gardens.

Hadrian's villa at Tivoli can lay claim to being the most influential of classical water gardens. Built between AD 118 and 138, the emperor's rural retreat drew on an abundant local water supply to service a collection of water features that included a recreation of the Canopus river in Egypt, and the Emperor's inner sanctum – a circular island surrounded by a moat.

Using Hadrian's creation as their inspiration, Italian Renaissance gardens were packed with fantastical fountains, grottoes and statues. In Mannerist pleasure gardens such as the Villa d'Este in Tivoli, and Hellbrunn Palace near Salzburg, water engaged all the senses: visitors could enjoy the classical references (Ovid's *Metamorphoses* was a favourite source), hydro-powered automata, surround-sound cascades, as well as the frisson of a sudden surprise soaking, delivered by concealed water jets.

Water management can be tricky. At Versailles the demand for water was so immense that even the might of the Machine of Marly could not raise enough from the Seine to run all the palace fountains simultaneously. Inaugurated in 1684 and seven years in the making, the machine could pump a million gallons of water a day from the Seine.

Specialist *fontainiers* ensured that the waterworks at Versailles did exactly that, while the doyen of English landscapers, Capability Brown, was also an expert waterscaper, creating at properties such as Blenheim Palace naturalistic 'rivers' from dammed-up streams and lakes, in whose tranquil expanses an exquisite Palladian bridge might be perfectly reflected. William Kent's cascade at Chiswick House never worked in his lifetime, although his rill at Rousham House was better behaved and is revered today as an aquatic incarnation of Hogarth's serpentine 'line of beauty'.

Maintaining complex water features is expensive. The cost of restoring the Latona fountain at Versailles to celebrate the 300th anniversary of Louis XIV's death in 2015, for example, ran into millions of euros. No wonder Reginald Farrer's advice to would-be water gardeners in 1908 was simply, 'Don't'.

GLASSHOUSES

The **REPEAL** *of the* **GLASS TAX** *in* 1845, *and
the genius of Sir Joseph Paxton, transformed
the aristocratic conservatory and brought
the* **GREENHOUSE** *within the reach of*
ORDINARY GARDENERS.

Until the development of cylinder sheet glass in the nineteenth century and the repeal of the glass tax, glasshouses had been an expensive proposition. Classically styled orangeries were an early incarnation of the glasshouse, providing frost-free winter quarters for costly containerized citrus trees. Royalty led the way: the orangery at Versailles, designed by Jules Hardouin-Mansart in 1684 for Louis XIV, extends to 150 metres (490 feet), with room for hundreds of plants.

Heated 'stove houses' accommodated tender crops such as peaches, grapes and, most prized and exotic of all, pineapples. Pineries

became a feature of country estates such as Chatsworth House, where a pineapple house was built in 1738. 'Vinery-pineries' combined grape and pineapple culture, and specialist heated quarters were also built for camellias, introduced from the Far East in the eighteenth century.

Chatsworth boasted numerous glasshouses, thanks to the plant-mad 6th Duke of Devonshire and his multitalented head gardener Joseph Paxton, whose 'Great Stove' was completed in 1840. At 70 metres (227 feet) long and 20 metres (67 feet) high, it had a two-lane central carriageway and different climatic zones, heated by eight coal-fired boilers.

Paxton went on to mastermind the Crystal Palace, that cast-iron-and-glass mothership of Victorian glasshouses, built for the 1851 Great Exhibition and whose structure was inspired by the Amazonian waterlily (for which Paxton had, naturally, designed a glasshouse at Chatsworth in 1849).

Cast iron technology had its benefits – its narrow glazing bars and large spans let the light flood in – but also drawbacks. The humid conditions enjoyed by tropical plants are inimical to wood and iron; iconic Victorian glasshouses, such as the Palm House and the Temperate House at Kew Gardens, have needed major restoration in recent years.

At Crystal Palace, Paxton used prefabrication to speed construction, a concept that also underpinned his 'Hothouses for the Millions' range of flat-packed, modular wooden-framed glasshouses. Of 'unparalleled cheapness', these allowed ordinary householders to garden under glass. Aluminium frames became standard in twentieth-century domestic greenhouses, with the democratization of growing under cover completed by the post-war arrival of inexpensive polytunnels, which replaced the hazards of brittle, millimetre-thin horticultural glass with polythene sheeting.

Where once glasshouse design took its cue from traditional post-and-lintel architecture, a more futuristic approach also emerged in the twentieth century. The Climatron, the first conservatory to be based on Richard Buckminster Fuller's space-efficient geodesic system, opened at the Missouri Botanical Garden in 1960. Forty years on, at the Eden Project, soap-bubble clusters of geodesic domes combine to create two huge biomes, whose structures are glazed with the polymer ETFE, or 'clingfilm with attitude'.

DRY
GARDENING

Counterintuitive it may sound, but
GARDENING WITHOUT WATER *is*
possible. Dry gardening, or XERISCAPING,
uses DROUGHT-TOLERANT *plants and*
mulches to reduce or eliminate the need for
watering – as pioneered by such advocates as
Beth Chatto in the UK.

The Ancient Mariner may have had a point. Although almost three-quarters of the Earth's surface is covered with water, only 1 per cent of it is readily accessible as fresh water. Water, although seemingly everywhere, is in increasingly short supply, as climate change, urbanization and population growth put pressure on a finite resource.

Even the UK, with its reputation for precipitation, cannot afford to waste water; it has less water available per capita than many of its European neighbours, and London receives less rainfall than Istanbul. The growing need to reduce domestic water consumption extends to gardens, whose traditional array of lawn, ornamental beds, hanging baskets and containers require more than a drop of H_2O to drink.

Rainwater harvesting, grey-water recycling, Mediterranean plants, mulching and even horror letting the lawn go brown – are now widely promoted options for those gardening in the face of water-usage restrictions, or an ever-ticking water meter. Cultivating a dry garden is a more sustainable option long-term, particularly in southeast England, the UK's driest and most water-stressed region. Since 1960 Beth Chatto has pioneered 'ecological' gardening at her garden in Essex (average annual rainfall 609 mm [24 inches]).

By looking at where plants grow in the wild, and choosing tough, drought-adapted species over supposedly 'garden worthy' cultivars, Chatto has succeeded in creating a dry garden that works with its environment, while still being attractive.

Preaching inspiration, not irrigation, Chatto's book *The Dry Garden* was published in 1978 (two years after the drought of 1976 had introduced a nation to water rationing and hosepipe bans), and in 1991/92 she created a gravel garden on the site of an old car park, whose soil was so poor that even native weeds would not grow there. True to the original intention of the garden, it has thrived, despite having never been watered.

Amenity horticulture has also woken up to the ecological benefits of dry gardening, and its reputation for low maintenance. Well suited to arid city environments, drought-tolerant green roofs and prairie-style herbaceous 'meadows' have become associated with the University of Sheffield's Department of Landscape, whose professors Nigel Dunnett and James Hitchmough worked on the planting design of the Olympic Park in London.

In desert areas of North America, xeriscaping is high on the agenda for local authorities and water companies. Demonstration gardens have proliferated since the 1980s, with sites such as the Tucson Botanical Gardens, and the Glendale Xeriscape Botanical Garden showcasing xeriscaping principles, along with native examples of the 'right plant for the right place' for desert gardens. Arizona's gardeners could not ask for a bigger hint of what they should be growing – their state flower is the blossom of the saguaro cactus (*Carnegiea gigantea*), the US's largest cactus.

ROCKERIES

The 'RIGHT PLANT IN THE RIGHT PLACE' is
a mantra that's DRUMMED into gardeners at every
opportunity but what to do if the plant in question
hails from HALFWAY UP A MOUNTAIN?

The answer is to provide alpine plants ('these austere little people of the hill', as the kingpin of Edwardian rock gardening Reginald Farrer called them) with a free-draining alp of their own. So, rockeries were created. One of Europe's oldest rock gardens is in the Chelsea Physic Garden, built in 1773 from assorted chalk, flint and corals, and Icelandic lava (originally brought to England as ship's ballast).

The nineteenth century saw some gardeners go to extraordinary lengths to achieve the ideal alpine condtions. In the 1830s Lady Broughton was in the vanguard with her 1-acre recreation of Chamonix at Hoole House in Cheshire, while the centrepiece of Sir Frank Crisp's 3-acre rockery at Friar Park was a 9-metre (30-foot) scale replica of the Matterhorn, complete with model mountain goats and a huge collection of some 4,000 alpine plant varieties.

But prior to the advent of alpine tourism in the mid-nineenth century, alpines were not widely grown – the rock garden installed at the Chelsea Physic Garden in the late eighteenth century was more in the way of an experimental garden. Other early rock gardens focused on creating dramatic landscape features, such as the Rock Garden and Strid at Chatsworth, conjured out of locally quarried stone by Joseph Paxton for the 6th Duke of Devonshire in the 1840s.

Authorities such as William Robinson and Reginald Farrer advocated the natural look, but artificial stone was widely used. The premier company for 'rockwork' was James Pulham and Son of Broxbourne, whose proprietary mixture of Portland cement, clinker and brick could be cast or modelled to resemble sandstone or limestone, and was much lighter than the real thing, 'Pulhamite' was used in the royal rock gardens at Sandringham House in the 1870s, and later at Buckingham Palace (1904), as well as in large-scale municipal schemes at seaside resorts such as Margate and Folkstone.

The rock garden went mainstream in the twentieth century, thanks in part to authors such as Farrer, whose 1907 book *My Rock Garden* went into many editions, and B. H. B. Symons-Jeune, whose 1932 *Natural Rock*

Gardening explained how to arrange rock gardens with geological fidelity. Prestigious, publicly accessible rock gardens, such as the one at RHS Wisley (built in 1910/12) also played their part, as did the seductive power of the Chelsea Flower Show, where rock gardens were a staple from after World War I up until their fall from grace in the 1960s.

The interwar popularity of rock gardens was reflected in the formation of the Alpine Garden Society in 1929, and the proliferation of specialist nurseries such as Ingwersens and Six Hills. Innovative, small-scale methods for growing alpines in dry stone walls, raised beds, homemade hypertufa troughs or in the cracks of crazy paving further democratized the rock garden.

No longer a must-have, rock gardens have nevertheless continued to evolve. 'Crevice gardens' are the latest incarnation; developed by Czech gardeners in the 1990s, these are characterized by narrow planting crevices between vertically arranged stones. In 2012, a modern crevice rock garden was unveiled at RHS Wisley to celebrate the centenary of its original rock garden.

TOPIARY

Topiary or not topiary, that has been the **QUESTION** *for gardeners over the centuries. The* **ART OF SCULPTING** *evergreen plants dates back to at least the Roman era. Pliny the Elder attributed the invention of topiary to* **GAIUS MARTIUS** *during the reign of Augustus. First laid out by* **GUILLAUME BEAUMONT** *in 1694,* **LEVENS HALL** *in Cumbria is reputed to be the world's oldest surviving topiary garden.*

For eighteenth-century landscape gardeners the answer was very firmly 'not topiary'. Only royal command dissuaded Capability Brown from ripping out the yew maze at Hampton Court during his tenure there, while influential commentators such as Alexander Pope and Thomas Addison ridiculed the pretentions and artificiality of topiary. Writing in 1712 Addison declared, 'I would rather look upon a tree in all its luxuriance and diffusion of boughs and branches, than when it is thus cut and trimmed into a mathematical figure'.

Pope and Addison were reacting against the highly formal Franco-Dutch style of gardening exemplified by royal gardens such as Versailles and Het Loo. At Versailles hundreds of topiaries defined and punctuated the grand perspectives and symmetrical

parterres created by André Le Nôtre in the 1600s. Dozens of shapes were possible, whose pompoms irresistibly call to mind the poodles popular with the French royal family. In 1745, Louis XV attended a ball at Versailles dressed as a yew topiary, and in this guise successfully wooed the future Madame de Pompadour.

The ur-topiarists of the Roman Empire, by contrast, enjoyed the creative challenge of figurative subjects. Pliny the Elder included descriptions of cypress trees clipped into naval and hunting scenes in *Natural History*, while his nephew, Pliny the Younger, owned a garden populated by 'figures of animals cut in box', which was tended by a specialist gardening slave, the topiarus.

Formal topiary experienced a revival in the nineteenth century, and was used on a grand scale in the Renaissance-style garden at Villandry and at Marqueyssac, which was planted with thousands of box tree plants (today there are 150,000), clipped into hummocks to echo the surrounding Dordogne hills.

Whimsical, narrative topiary enlivened interwar gardens in the twentieth century. Lady Londonderry's topiary at Mount Stewart depicted characters from Irish mythology, while the topiaries created by Harvey S. Ladew at his garden in Maryland in the 1930s included a full-on hunting scene with fox, hounds and riders hurtling across the lawn. Ever adaptable, formal topiary has more recently found a place in Modernist gardens, such as those designed by the Belgian landscape architect Jacques Wirtz.

Formal or figurative, topiary requires patience and skill. At Levens Hall the huge historic topiaries take months to shear into shape, despite labour-saving power tools and cherrypickers. In Japan, gardeners practising the art of sculpting – or cloud pruning – their garden trees (*niwaki*) complete a seven-year apprenticeship before flying solo with their shears.

CARPET BEDDING

The **ANTITHESIS** *of* **LOW-MAINTENANCE**
*gardening, carpet bedding provides colourful
massed displays of, usually, tender plants, arranged to
form complex patterns.* **A LABOUR-INTENSIVE**
approach, carpet bedding became **ALL THE RAGE**
with Victorian gardeners.

The term was coined around 1868 by the *Gardeners' Chronicle*, while the technique was pioneered at grand Victorian gardens such as Waddesdon Manor. It involved masses of plants, selected for their vividly coloured flowers or contrasting foliage, planted closely together to create an unbroken surface, and arranged in patterns, symbols or words. A linear variant, ribbon planting, uses contrasting bands of flowering plants to create flowing rivers of colour along a border's edge.

Perfected by head gardeners at stately piles such as Cliveden, Waddesdon and Cragside, carpet bedding schemes were a re-imagining of seventeenth-century parterres, and became a status symbol requiring anything from 10,000 to 40,000 plants for a showy display. It was a very different aesthetic from the single exotic specimens displayed in reverential isolation by Georgian gardeners, or the naturalist 'wild' gardens advocated by William Robinson.

John Fleming, Cliveden's head gardener, is credited as the inventor of carpet bedding; he designed the box-edged parterre there in 1855. Some gardeners constructed mounded

beds to allow floral patterns to be more visible, and at Waddesdon Manor the technique was also applied to 3D garden sculptures. Restored by the National Trust in the 1990s, the parterre at Waddesdon still features twice-yearly displays of carpet bedding and floral sculptures.

A perfect alignment of circumstances made this planting profusion possible: the abundance of new plant material arriving from around the world throughout the nineteenth century, the repeal of the glass tax in 1845 and the window tax in 1851 (allowing greater quantities of summer bedding to be raised under glass), and a skilled horticultural workforce. Popular carpet bedding plants include easy-to-trim foliage specimens such as *Alternanthera*, *Echeveria*, *Sedum* and *Sempervivum*, and floriferous plants like *Iberis*, wall flowers, forget-me-nots, marigolds, *Pelargonium*, heliotropes and *Salvia*. Schemes have to be changed at least twice a year (tender summer bedding is planted out at the end of spring in May, followed by hardy bedding in October).

What started as an exclusive pursuit of the rich was soon adopted in the modest gardens of the masses (more rag rug than Persian carpet, perhaps) and over-the-top bedding displays also became a staple of civic horticulture. In the current era of budget cuts, the Carpet Gardens at the British seaside resort of Eastbourne are a rare survivor. Dating from 1880, they are still densely planted in true carpet style, using 400 plants per square metre. Floral clocks are a distinct subspecies of the genre; the Horloge Fleurie in Geneva has celebrated the town's watchmaking tradition since 1955, and there has been a floral clock at Niagara Park, Ontario, since 1950, requiring up to 16,000 plants, changed twice yearly.

Modern carpet bedding is no less labour and plant-intensive than its Victorian forebear, although layouts are now usually designed on a computer. Once considered the height of horticultural sophistication, carpet bedding's subsequent reputation for kitsch is perhaps best summed up by Jeff Koons's outsized floral sculpture *Puppy* (1992), now guarding the Guggenheim Museum in Bilbao.

CLIMATE CHANGE

Climate change presents opportunities as well as challenges for twenty-first-century gardeners, who more than ever before have to plan for **DISRUPTIVE WEATHER EVENTS**, from **DROUGHT** to **DELUGE**. New types of gardens have been developed in response, and **TRADITIONAL LAWNS** and **HERBACEOUS BORDERS** may yet become **THINGS OF THE PAST**.

Working with the seasons is one of gardening's greatest pleasures, and one of its most exacting necessities. Before climate change as we know it, gardeners simply coped with 'weather' – its heat waves, hailstorms and uncalled cold snaps (London's 'Great Frost' of 1683–84 destroyed many of diarist John Evelyn's treasured tender plants, as he ruefully recorded).

These days things are hotting up in our gardens – literally. The global mean surface temperature has risen by 0.86°C (1.53°F) since 1880, and 2016 was the warmest year on record to date. Over the past decade, the UK

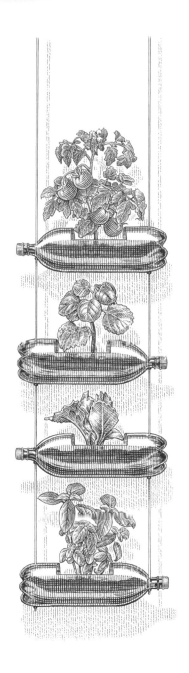

growing season has lengthened by nearly a month, encouraging non-native diseases and pests, such as heuchera rust and rosemary beetle (both recent arrivals in the UK), and the prospect of gardens that need year-round maintenance.

Even climate change has changed. In 2002, the RHS envisaged that the UK would come to bask in a Mediterranean climate, and suggested a planting palette of olive trees, lavender and rosemary in anticipation. Their 2017 report *Gardening in a Changing Climate* revised this appealing prediction, replacing it with a forecast of extreme weather events – droughts, heavy rains and stronger winds – set against the backdrop of rising global temperatures, exacerbated by urbanization.

Gardeners are now being urged to capture carbon in their gardens by avoiding unsustainable peat-based composts and by installing features such as rain gardens and green roofs. Developed in the US in the 1990s, rain gardens relieve the pressure on mains drains by slowing water run-off from roofs while filtering out pollutants before they reach watercourses. By using plants that can withstand droughts as well as periods of waterlogging, rain gardens can absorb up to 30 per cent more water than a lawn. Kerbside rain gardens – such as the one designed by Nigel Dunnett for John Lewis's HQ in central London – tackle the problem of run-off caused by the proliferation of paved surfaces in urban areas.

As well as mitigating water run-off, green roofs are being deployed to reduce the urban heat island effect (UHIE), a phenomenon in which buildings and hard surfaces absorb and release the sun's heat, creating urban microclimates. Like rain gardens, green roofs intercept run-off, allow moisture to evaporate, lower the temperature and improve air quality by converting CO_2 into oxygen. Paris – hit hard by heatwaves in 2003 and 2006 – is aiming to increase its green space by 100,000 hectares by 2020, with green roofs and walls being part of that strategy.

Domestic gardeners are also encouraged to do their bit by reducing their reliance on products and materials whose manufacture comes at a high carbon cost. Recycling, reduction of waste and the repurposing of unwanted objects and packaging are among the ways gardeners can help the climate every day.

Facing up to the effects of climate change, botanic gardens safeguard biodiversity by conserving plants in living collections and in seed banks. But climate change threatens even these, as the 2016 leakage of permafrost melt water into the entrance tunnel of the Svalbard Global Seed Bank in Norway demonstrated only too vividly.

RUS IN URBE
THE GARDEN SQUARE

Part **PUBLIC PARK**, *part* **COMMUNAL GARDEN**,
*the enclosed garden square originated in Europe, but became
a particular feature of* **RESIDENTIAL DEVELOPMENTS**
in Georgian and Victorian London.

A kind of popular *hortus conclusus*, the London garden square took its initial inspiration from European squares such as the Place des Vosges in Paris. Perhaps it was inevitable that the British, with their obsession with gardens and landscapes, would want to inject some rural charm into this most urbane of town-planning types. The first square in London to be planned around a garden is reckoned to be Soho Square, whose pleasure grounds were laid out in the late 1670s on land owned by the Earl of St Albans. Other aristocratic families followed suit, and the names of those upmarket developers live on in the elegant,

fashionable residential squares that they built on their London estates from the late seventeenth century onwards: Bedford, Portman, Grosvenor, Bedford, Russell, Cadogan …

London's squares were originally part of a suburban expansion, and often built over distinctly bucolic features, such as Markham Square, SW3 (which was on the site of an orchard), or leisure amenities, as in the case of Ladbroke Square Garden (laid out in 1849 on the site of the Hippodrome racecourse).

The garden element of garden squares seems to have taken a bit of time to get going – contemporary engravings of newly built squares often depict rather stark layouts of plain grass 'plats' surrounded by railings or a regimented line of trees. Spotting a missed opportunity, Thomas Fairchild (he of the Mule) promoted the *rus in urbe* (countryside in the city) ideal in his 1722 publication *The City Gardener*, in which he advocated laying squares out in the 'Rural Manner', and pointed out both the wildlife and aesthetic benefits of doing so. The Hoxton nurseryman even ventured his own design for a square, featuring paths radiating from a central circular mount, planted with trees.

Landscape designers more usually associated with large country estates also helped bring a rustic vibe to the city squares. Charles Bridgeman and John Nash were successively involved in St James's Square, while Humphry Repton worked on Russell Square and Cadogan Place Gardens. The elements that became the hallmark of London's garden squares were put into place: plantations of pollution tolerant trees such as limes or planes, privacy-providing shrubberies, winding walkways, and lawns. Modern amenities such as tennis courts and children's play areas followed in due course.

Valued, as Fairchild foresaw, as important pieces in the jigsaw of parks and gardens that make London's green corridor, garden squares are protected by act of parliament. Although squares such as Russell Square and Bloomsbury Square are open to the public, many remain as private communal gardens, open to key-holding residents only, with railings and locked gates having become a feature of garden squares from quite early on. Every June, dozens of London's garden squares open their gates as part of the Open Garden Squares Weekend, to allow the public the opportunity to experience these urban Edens, along with the traditional garden-visiting pleasures of tea and cake in a festive atmosphere.

THE HA-HA

The ha-ha is SYNONYMOUS *with
eighteenth-century English landscape garden –
particularly those created by* CHARLES
BRIDGEMAN, WILLIAM KENT *and, later,*
LANCELOT 'CAPABILITY' BROWN.

Placed at the end of a lawn, this deceptively
simple ditch-and-wall arrangement magical-
ly blurred the boundary between garden and
field, allowing the illusion that the landscape
was as one with the garden. More prosaically,
the 'sunk fence' also unobtrusively prevented
livestock from straying into the garden, while
simultaneously providing a source of amuse-
ment (hence the name) for unsuspecting visitors once they discovered the device.

One of the oldest ha-has in Britain is
that at Levens Hall, which was in existence
by 1695, installed by Guillaume Beaumont,
one-time gardener to James II. The origins
of the ha-ha, however, predate the advent of
the new-fangled profession of 'landscape designer', the utilitarian ditch having long been
used as a stock-proof fence, while medieval
saltatoria or deer leaps also combined a ditch
and wall to keep deer from straying.

Although Charles Bridgeman is wrongly
credited (by Horace Walpole) as the creator
of the ha-ha as a garden feature, he did help
popularize it; his ha-ha at Stowe dates from
1719 and is over 6 kilometres (4 miles) long.
The diarist John Evelyn saw it in 1725 and got
the concept instantly ('there being no walls to
be seen, the prospect of the country is very
extensive'). The ha-ha at Stowe also made
an impression on the naturalist and gardener
Gilbert White, who, following a visit, set
about installing one on a more domestic scale
at his house in Selbourne over the winter of
1760/61. Although his workmen (who were
paid a grand total of £1, 8s, 10d for their labours) ended up sinking the ditch deeper
than intended, White was pleased with the
result. It was, he wrote, 'An excellent fence
against the mead, and so well fastned into
the clay bank, that it looks likely to stand a
long while.' He was right: his ha-ha (although
restored in 2000) still overlooks the parkland
beyond his garden.

The ha-ha was a staple of the grand coun-
try-house landscapes designed by Capability
Brown, examples of which can be seen at Petworth House (where the ha-ha keeps the deer
out rather than in), and at Burghley House.
The ha-ha at Burghley has recently been restored, the 300-metre (985-foot) limestone
stretch requiring the removal of 2,500 tonnes
of material, and taking a painstaking 12 years
to complete.

In his essay 'On Modern Gardening',
Horace Walpole recorded the ha-ha's revo-
lutionary effect, wittily describing it as 'the
leading step to all that followed' and not-
ing its transformative effect on the relation-
ship between garden and countryside: 'No
sooner than this simple enchantment made,
than levelling, mowing and rolling, followed.
The contiguous ground of the park without
the sunk fence was to be harmonized with
the lawn within; and the garden in its turn
was to be set free from its prim regularity,
that it might assort with the wilder country
without.' The ha-ha was, therefore, essential
to the Arcadian vision.

HORTICULTURAL
SOCIETIES

The first horticultural societies in England were set up in the seventeenth century by 'florists', **ENTHUSIASTS** *who bred a small range of flowers for competition. Over the centuries, the societies have broadened their remit* **BEYOND THE BLOOM** *to include all kinds of garden produce, and their competitions take place at everything from the local* **VILLAGE FETE** *to national horitcultural shows.*

Florists' societies were introduced (it is believed) by Flemish émigré weavers. The Ancient Society of York Florists, the world's oldest surviving horticultural society, was founded in 1768. Traditionally, florists focused their efforts on just six flowers – hyacinths, auriculas, polyanthus, ranunculus, carnations and tulips – but in the nineteenth century, this narrow repertoire expanded to include pinks, dahlias and chrysanthemums. The focus of sustained hybridization, florists' flowers evolved into distinct types, the ball-shaped English florists' tulips with their flamed and feathered markings, for example, becoming quite different from their Dutch relations.

Conviviality and competition were the twin pillars of the florists' societies, which held shows for each flower type from April through to August, starting with auriculas. With prizes and breeding deals to be won, rivalry was fierce, but shows were sociable events that were usually held in pubs and followed by a 'feast', a slap-up meal with alcohol very much on the menu. It is perhaps no coincidence that the Wakefield and North of England Tulip Society (England's last remaining specialist tulip society) exhibit their blooms in brown beer bottles.

The florists' zealous pursuit of progress (and love of a good flower show) was shared by professional horticulturalists. In 1804 Joseph Banks and William Forsyth were among the founder members of the Horticultural Society of London, which became the Royal Horticultural Society in 1861. The society's aim of improving the 'science, art and practice of horticulture' translated into sponsoring plant-hunting missions around the world, setting up professional exams for gardeners, and opening experimental gardens at Chiswick and Kensington.

RHS plant trials continue today at the regional gardens the society established throughout the twentieth century; many are held at its principal garden in Wisley (acquired in 1903), sometimes in conjunction with specialist groups such as the Sweet Pea Society. The RHS 'Award of Garden Merit' was introduced in 1922 to denote particularly garden-worthy plants. Plants, and the nurseries that grow them, are put under further scrutiny at RHS flower shows, the most prestigious of which, the Chelsea Flower Show, began life as the 'Great Spring Show' in 1862, housed in a single tent.

With their aspirational show gardens and look-but-don't-touch floral displays, flower shows are the haute couture of horticulture. Nurseries debut their most promising new plants at flower shows – the poinsettia was first introduced to American gardeners at the inaugural Philadelphia Flower Show in 1829, while stalwarts such as *Geranium* 'Rozanne', *Erysimum* 'Bowles's Mauve' and *Rosa* 'Iceberg' are some of the outstanding plants to have been introduced at Chelsea Flower Show since 1913. Flower shows have long been places to discover the latest design trends, with Chelsea's designer gardens prefiguring the rise of the rock garden and the repurposing of gardens as sociable 'outdoor rooms'.

At a regional level, local horticultural societies offer their members a programme of talks by guest speakers, garden visits, seed swaps and plant sales, often culminating in a hotly contested flower and produce show at the end of the summer.

GARDENERS' ALMANACS

—⟶ѮѮ⟵—

Part instruction manual, part aide-memoire, the gardener's calendar or almanac is an
EVERGREEN STAPLE *of gardening literature. One of the first month-by-month manuals*
in English of these seasonal guides to **WHAT TO DO IN THE GARDEN, AND WHEN,**
was John Evelyn's Kalendarium Hortense; or, *the* Gard'ners Almanac, *first published*
in 1664 and running to many editions.

𝓨

Roman agricultural writers included gardening in their dos and don'ts of estate management. Columella, writing in the first century AD, devoted a whole book to it with his multi-volume work *De Re Rustica*. Columella covered the gardening year and contained instructions on soil preparation, pest control and what plant varieties to sow.

Roman agronomists were still being consulted well into the Renaissance era by writers such as Thomas Hill, whose mid-sixteenth-century book, the catchily titled *A most brief and pleasaunte treatise teachynge how to dresse, sowe and set a garden*, was the first gardening book to be published in English. Despite its derivative content, it ran to several editions, as did Hill's subsequent book, *The Gardener's Labyrinth*. Published posthumously in 1577, this illustrated manual contained 'instructions for the choice of seedes, apt times for

sowing, setting, planting and watering', as well as ideas for laying out knot gardens, mazes and herb gardens.

Published in 1664 as an appendix to *Sylva*, his great work on trees, John Evelyn's *Kalendarium Hortense* offered a month-by-month to-do list in the orchard, kitchen garden, parterre and flower garden, along with lists of which fruit and flowers would be at their best. The tone is brisk and authoritative, and palpably written from personal experience. Evelyn, a leading figure of the English Enlightenment and a founder member of the Royal Society, was a knowledgeable gardener, putting his ideas into practice over many years in his garden at Sayes Court, in Deptford.

Evelyn's almanac set the bar for future calendars and is still worth consulting today (remembering that Evelyn was working from the Julian calendar, rather than the

Gregorian). It provides a roster of tasks for the whole garden year, including manuring, sowing, propagation, weed-killing (a July job, using salt water, potash and tobacco) and on-going 'hostilities' against vermin. There are instructions on using hot beds to get 'fine and tender seeds' off to an early start, and remind-ers to protect crops against the cold.

A century later, 'best modern practice' informs John Abercrombie's 1767 tome *Every Man his Own Gardener*. A gardener by pro-fession, Abercrombie's book included not just what to do each month and when, but also the nitty-gritty of how. Detailed instructions on 'the method of proceeding', crop by crop, en-sured that it was still in print at least 50 years after its author's death in 1806.

While Abercrombie's book was pitched at 'gentlemen and young professors', Mrs Lou-don's *The Amateur Gardener's Calendar* (1847) provided practical guidance for recreational gardeners. As well as offering guidance on the when, what and how of the gardening year, the doyenne of Victorian gardening literature innovatively instructed on 'things not to be done', saving her enthusiastic amateur readers from rookie errors such as pruning in frosty weather or digging up their tulips too soon.

Each age gets the gardening calendar it needs. Mrs Loudon's advised on that most Victorian of garden features, the shrubbery, and how best to apply the miracle fertilizer of the age, guano. During World War II, the BBC's radio gardener C. H. Middleton helped the population dig for victory with his month-by-month guides such as *Your Garden in War-Time* (1941) and *Digging for Victory* (1942).

Gardeners' almanacs continue into the digital age: the RHS website can be consult-ed at the click of a mouse, and many online plant suppliers also offer month-by-month advice on what to do in the garden – as well as advice on what to buy, of course.

NO-DIG GARDENING

A **LESS-IS-MORE** *approach to soil cultivation that avoids traditional digging in favour of* **MULCHING** *and allowing* **MICRO-ORGANISMS** *in the soil to break down organic matter naturally.*

'Bastard trenching' – or double digging, as it is more politely known – is so-named for a reason. It is hard graft and, if not done cor-rectly, a sure-fire way of picking up a back injury. But gardeners have been digging for centuries, faithfully following the received wisdom that cultivation aerates the soil, al-lows organic matter to be incorporated into it, and brings pests to the surface.

It was not until the mid twentieth century that F. C. King, the head gardener of Levens Hall, posed the provocative question 'Is Dig-ging Necessary?', in a pamphlet published in 1946. A disciple of the Indore method of composting, King started his experiments with no digging as early as 1920, inspired by his observations of wild garlic flourishing in uncultivated soil. By 'resting the spade' and applying regular applications of compost to the soil, King discovered he could get good yields from fruit and veg crops, and with noticeably fewer aphid infestations.

King recognized that no dig represented 'a drastic overhaul of traditional practice', but the idea gained credibility. In the 1970s, no dig got big with popular how-to guides such as Ruth Stout's *No-Work Gardening Book* in America, and Esther Deans's *Growing without Digging* in Australia. And in 1978, Japanese agricultural scientist Masanobu Fukuoka published his bestselling 'do nothing' farming manifesto, *One-Straw Revolution*. A hero of the permaculture movement, Fukuoka took no dig to even further extremes, with a hands-off farming method that also prohibited pruning, weeding, and fertilizers and pesticides. More recently, British organic-vegetable grower Charles Dowding, a non-digger since 1983, has promoted no-dig growing through courses and books on the subject.

The no-dig philosophy is an organic, soil-centric approach to gardening that deems digging to be detrimental to soil health. Far from being beneficial, digging can harm valuable micro-organisms and mycorrhizae, damage the soil structure and encourage erosion, while also killing earthworms and bringing weed seeds to the surface. Instead of cultivating the soil, no-diggers apply regular mulches of organic matter (such as compost, manure, leaves, twigs, grass cuttings, straw and even cardboard), increasing the depth of top soil and allowing worms and micro-organisms to become incorporated naturally into the soil. No dig is also promoted as saving time and labour (although turning compost heaps is arguably just as laborious as digging, and potentially just as injurious to backs).

No dig works well with raised vegetable beds (where it avoids the need for the gardener to trample the soil while working it); it is perhaps less suitable for herbaceous borders or mixed borders where plants need to be regularly lifted and divided.

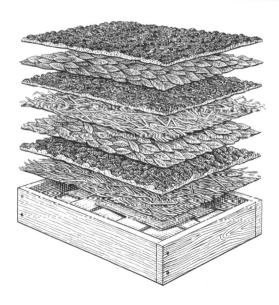

AERIAL AND VERTICAL GARDENS

With land at a premium in cities, for some gardens the only way is up. SPACE-EFFICIENT *vertical gardens offer environmental as well as aesthetic benefits, although their* SPECIALIST MAINTENANCE *requirements can present* CHALLENGES.

Gardening above street level is nothing new: in the mid-1930s British landscape architect Ralph Hancock made a name for himself with the roof gardens he designed in New York and London. His 'Garden of the Nations' at the Rockefeller Centre boasted gardens in the Japanese, Spanish, Dutch, Italian and English styles, and was an aerial undertaking that involved some 2,000 trees and thousands of tonnes of earth being hauled up to the eleventh floor by the service lift, or block and tackle.

While traditional roof gardens rely on soil as a growing medium, today's vertical gardens harness hydroponic technology. Requiring minimal or no soil, these lightweight growing systems can be applied to interior or exterior walls and offer the visual amenity of a garden while insulating the host building, improving air quality and boosting biodiversity.

Such 'living walls' were pioneered by the French botanist and plant hunter Patrick Blanc from the late 1980s. His observations of plants growing freely without soil in limestone cliffs and jungle trees inspired his system of growing plants in synthetic felt pockets, their nutritional needs being met by hydroponics. Blanc has since installed hundreds of *murs végétals* around the world, including at the Musée du Quai Branly in Paris, whose exotic scheme of plants from China, Japan and the Americas echoes the non-European focus of the museum's ethnographic collections.

Successful vertical gardening demands the right plant in the right place. The site's altitude, as well as its orientation, must be considered, with shade loving plants typically positioned lower down the building, and drought-tolerant, wind-resistant specimens at the top. Pollution, exposure and desiccating winds can be fatal, and all vertically grown plants, whether exterior or interior, are at the mercy of temperamental automatic watering systems and inexpert maintenance.

With easy-to-install, pre-grown modular systems now available, vertical gardens have become a form of public art, gracing hotels, shopping centres and building-site hoardings; in 2011 the National Gallery in London even hosted a living-wall rendition of Van Gogh's painting *Wheatfield, with Cypresses.*

Vertical gardening continues to evolve, creatively and technically. Singapore's recent efforts to become 'a city in a garden' include a grove of giant artificial trees, whose 'trunks' are planted with a biodiverse mix of species. In Milan, the audacious Bosco Verticale designed by architect Stefano Boeri integrates around 900 trees on the cantilevered balconies of its two high-rise apartment blocks.

KNOT GARDENS
AND
PARTERRES

—⁂—

A formal style of garden popular in the Tudor period, using low evergreen hedges to create **COMPLEX GEOMETRIC PATTERNS,** *or 'knots'. These later developed into the* **PARTERRES** *and* **BRODERIES** *of Baroque gardens.*

Tudor knot gardens took their cue from the highly patterned decorative arts of the period, using plants to replicate the flowing, foliate designs of carpets, plasterwork, tapestry and textiles. One of the earliest known images of a knot garden appears in a woodcut illustration in an early printed book, the courtly romance *The Dream of Polyphilus,* published in 1499 in Venice.

Like living embroideries, Tudor knot gardens had intertwining hedges of fragrant evergreen herbs such as rosemary, germander or cotton lavender, which could be clipped where the intertwining rows met, to give the impression of one thread superimposed over another. Box was used, but not everyone appreciated its distinctive cat's wee odour – John Gerald, author of the sixteenth-century *Herball,* did not mince his words when he called it an 'evil and loathsome' plant.

Small, solidly planted, self-contained knots were said to be 'closed', while their 'open' counterparts were larger, with space for paths and contrasting areas of gravel, brick or coloured sand between the hedges. The original year-round garden feature, knot gardens were expressions of man's mastery over nature, designed to be viewed from above, from a terrace or an artificial mound, or the upper storey of a house.

As ever, royalty and the nobility set the fashion; Henry VII's palace at Richmond is known to have featured 'royal knots, alleyed and herbed' in 1501. By 1577, books such as Thomas Hill's *The Gardener's Labyrinth* contained illustrations of knots for the less exalted to try at home. No original Tudor knots survive, but a revival of interest in historical garden styles in the 1980s led to some notable modern interpretations, such as those created by the Dowager Marchioness of Salisbury, whose knot garden at Hatfield House featured a historically correct planting palette of clipped box, yew, holly, santolina, phillyrea and, unusually, hawthorn.

Open knots evolved into the extensive parterres first laid out in the seventeenth century at Baroque palaces such as Vaux le Vicomte and Versailles in France, and Het Loo in Holland. The ornate scrolling patterns of contemporary embroidery continued to provide inspiration for the designs – to the extent that such gardens were known as parterre de broderie. Clipped box hedges and flower-filled borders now provided the edging detail, with decorative motifs cut out of grassy plots, or gazon coupé, set against gravel areas for contrast.

Like knot gardens, parterres were intended to be seen from a high viewpoint, and were often accompanied by viewing terraces. Later, Capability Brown (the man responsible for sweeping away such old-fashioned formality) complained that it was only nurserymaids tending their charges who benefited most from these aerial views.

THE GARDEN CENTRE

The concept of buying plants throughout the year from **OUT-OF-TOWN** 'garden centres' took off after World War II, coinciding with the development of **CONTAINER-GROWN** plants, mass motor-car ownership and a post-war **HOUSING BOOM**.

Before the advent of the garden centre, the business of buying plants was a strictly seasonal affair. Nurserymen supplied bare-rooted plants between October and March, often on a mail order basis. Gardeners had to wait until the 1960s for the age of instant gratification to dawn, in the form of container-grown plants, available year-round from a novel mutation of the nursery, the 'garden centre'. These new horticultural retailers (which often developed out of long-established nursery businesses) also sold fertilizers, pesticides, outdoor furniture and sundries – everything that the post-war gardener needed in one destination, with added car-parking.

Container-grown plants made the concept possible, particularly when light, easy-to-transport plastic polythene pots became widely available in the 1960s. An early UK proponent of this idea was Herefordshire nurseryman Harry Williamson (founder

of Wyevale Garden Centres), who, having seen container growing in America in the 1930s, experimented with growing roses in tin cans.

UK nurseries such as Stewarts, Notcutts and Wyevale were pioneers of container-plant retailing, with Edward Stewart opening the country's first garden centre at Ferndown, Dorset, in 1955, in converted potting sheds on the family nursery. Stewart had travelled to North America in 1953 and had realized that container plants retailed through a garden centre was the way for his business, practically bankrupted by wartime depredations, to survive. In 1961 Stewart set up a second, purpose-built, out-of-town garden centre, complete with coffee shop, in Christchurch, with BBC TV's gardening presenter Percy Thrower officially opening its doors to the public. The whole garden centre concept was given a royal seal of approval when the late

Queen Mother opened Syon Park Garden Centre in 1968. Thrower opened his own 'Gardening Centre' in 1970, in Shrewsbury.

The post-war suburban housing (and garden) boom provided a new customer base for the new garden centres, while the great British weather and industrial relations conspired against the traditional mail-order nursery business. The hard winter of 1963 froze plants into the ground from Christmas until March, meaning orders could not be dispatched (although presumably these would not have been able to have been planted even had they been delivered). By chance, Britain's first ever general post office strike also coincided with the bare root season, running from 20 January to 7 March 1971. Customers discovered the convenience and pleasure of buying container plants from garden centres with their attractive and colourful 'planterias' (another new concept), and by 1966 such was the popularity of garden centres that the Horticultural Trades Association had set up a Gardens Centre group.

Although garden centres changed the face of horticultural retailing, they have not killed off the mail-order side of things entirely. The internet has transformed the process of choosing and ordering plants, container-grown or otherwise, and a deregulated mail service has opened up delivery options. Field-grown, bare-root fruit trees and roses are still reckoned to be a better, more economic bet than their container-grown counterparts, and the success of internet nurseries such as Crocus (founded 2000) reveals that gardeners still have an appetite for plants delivered to their door, just like the good old days.

WOMEN
GARDENERS

Gardening became a popular amateur PASTIME
FOR LADIES *early in Queen Victoria's reign;*
by the end of the century, horticulture was
becoming an acceptable CAREER PATH *for her*
Empire's 'surplus' women.

❖

Gardening manuals written by women for women were published from the 1830s, with authors such as Louisa Johnson, Elizabeth Kent and Jane Loudon empowering their readers to discover the pleasures of hands-on horticulture.

A successful science-fiction author, Jane Webb was a gardening novice when she married the horticulturalist and writer John Claudius Loudon in 1830, but from a standing start she became a trusted authority as well as an accomplished botanic artist. As a self-taught gardener (she learned much by attending lectures given by the botanist John Lindley), Jane could identify with her female readers, whose education would typically have lacked science and Latin. Her first gardening book, *Instructions in Gardening for Ladies* (1840) sold 1,300 copies on the day of publication, and was followed by a steady succession

of bestselling 'ladies' titles, including *Botany for Ladies*.

Gardening as a profession opened up to women at the end of the century, with several horticultural schools catering exclusively for female pupils. Swanley Horticultural College in Kent accepted its first female students in 1891, and had become an all-female institution by the end of the century. Women regularly topped the exam boards and, despite scepticism in some quarters, in 1896 three Swanley graduates became the first women gardeners to work at Kew Gardens.

Horticulture was seen as a skill that unmarried emigrées could take to the colonies, but the move towards professionalism was not confined to Britain. In her 1908 book *Gardening for Women*, Frances Wolseley (founder of the Glynde School for Lady Gardeners), listed a number of other serious

establishments on the continent and in America (the Lowthorpe School of Landscape Architecture, Gardening, and Horticulture for Women in Massachusetts boasted the Olmsted brothers among its lecturers).

Even sceptics saw the point of professionally qualified female gardeners during the two world wars, when their objections (typically about women's perceived lack of physical strength), faded in the light of a national shortage of male gardeners and the urgent need for productive gardens. However, as with the case of so many women's wartime occupations, many female gardeners lost their jobs when peace returned. Beyond the world of private gardens however, female landscape designers such as Brenda Colvin and Sylvia Crowe (both Swanley graduates) helped shape the post-war world of campus universities, nuclear power stations and new towns.

Women garden makers have been among horticulture's most persuasive and enduring tastemakers. The doyenne of the herbaceous border, Gertrude Jekyll, and her contemporary, the incorrigible plantswoman Ellen Willmott, were the first women to be awarded the Victoria Medal, the RHS's highest honour, in 1897. With only 63 medals held at one time, the award is a telling barometer of contemporary horticulture; other influential figures to have been awarded the VM more recently include Rosemary Verey, Penelope Hobhouse, Beth Chatto and, in 2017, the 'queen of herbs', Jekka McVicar.

PLANT
CRAZES

*It is axiomatic that gardeners love plants, but some plants
seem to inspire more love than others. Every so often a kind of*
COLLECTIVE MADNESS *takes root, triggering an irresistible
urge to amass a particular species. The* **MANIA** *for rare and
beautiful* **TULIPS** *in seventeenth-century Holland was the*
FIRST PLANT CRAZE, *and fuelled frenzied speculation before
the bubble burst overnight in February 1637.*

What had begun as a gentlemanly trade among collectors in the sixteenth century turned into an overheated futures market in which a single bulb of a desirable 'broken' coloured variety, such as the red-and-white-streaked 'Semper Augustus', might be worth as much as a house, or a year's wages. Speculators gambling that their bulb would 'break' and become more valuable were working blind as colour breaks were unpredictable, the result of a virus only identified in the twentieth century.

Tulips, at least, were relatively easy to grow and propagate; orchids were another matter. In the early nineteenth century, gardeners struggled with the newly discovered tropical orchids. William Cattley's success in coaxing one such specimen into gorgeous flower in 1818 is credited with starting the

orchid craze; the orchid in question, *Cattleya labiata*, bears his name in recognition of this achievement.

Nurseries skilled in orchid cultivation, such as Loddiges in London, flourished, while the 'Orchid King' Frederick Sander helped popularize the plant by raising orchids by the million at his nurseries in England, America and Belgium. Others were less successful; such was the attrition rate in the early days that Joseph Banks described England as 'the grave of tropical orchids'. Some orchids' native habitats were rendered equally sepulchral at the hands of unscrupulous plant hunters, who would strip out entire populations of orchids rather than cede them to a rival.

Until botanists learned how to propagate orchids from seed, collecting was an elite hobby. The Duke of Devonshire was so smitten that he sent one of his own gardeners on a collecting mission to India and built the Great Stove at Chatsworth in expectation of his successful return (he duly introduced 100 new species). Today, orchids remain objects of desire, albeit ones readily available from the nearest supermarket.

The fern craze, which ran from the 1840s, was more egalitarian. Collections could be a couple of ferns in a Wardian case in a smoggy London terrace, or an entire valley recreated in a designated 'fernery', with Pulhamite grottoes and waterfalls, and stocked with exotic specimens such as *Dicksonia antarctica*. With 40 species native to Britain, collecting expeditions to Devon and other damp regions were popular, and since both sexes could participate in this improving activity together, romance might be on the cards as well. Primers such as Edward Newman's *A History of British Ferns* (1840) and Shirley Hibberd's *The Fern Garden* (1869) informed the amateur enthusiast, and ferns permeated the national consciousness, being reproduced on everything from umbrella stands to custard creams, but World War I signalled the end for full-blown pteridomania.

PARADISE
GARDENS

*From its foundation in the seventh century,
where* ISLAM *led,* GARDENS *followed. From*
PERSIA *to the* MUGHAL EMPIRE, *from the*
OTTOMAN EMPIRE *to North Africa, and
from thence to Al-Andalus in Spain and on,
in turn, to Mexico and California, the Islamic
garden became one of the most* WIDESPREAD
and INFLUENTIAL *garden types in the world.*

Its origins can be traced even further back in time, to the sixth century BC palace of Cyrus the Great at Pasargadae, in modern Iran. Excavations here have revealed a formal enclosed garden divided by stone-lined water channels – the template, some believe, for the distinctive quadripartite gardens created by the region's subsequent Persian conquerors, in which the garden is divided into four equal quarters by water rills set perpendicular to each other.

The four-garden (chahar bagh) layout of the Persian garden, with its life-giving and purifying water, easeful pavilions and its abundant shade- and fruit-giving trees, chimed with the Quranic vision of Paradise as a garden, flowing with the four rivers of life (milk, honey, water and wine). Persian gardens became known as paradise gardens (the word 'paradise' deriving from the old Persian *pairidaëza*, 'a walled park'), and a love of gardens permeated the culture, from specialist

garden poetry to the stylized recreations of plants and gardens in decorative arts such as ceramics and carpets.

Bringing water to these desert gardens was no mean feat. Brilliantly engineered gravity-fed underground *qanats*, or tunnels, brought water from distant aquifers to the site, where it was stored in cisterns or ponds before being distributed around the garden via irrigation channels. The land all around might be parched, yet within its defining walls, the garden was an oasis. But water, a scarce resource, was used with restraint. Drought-tolerant species such as cypresses, citruses, oleanders, myrtles, hollyhocks, roses and palms were set out in straight lines, for efficient watering. Centrally placed water features bubbled or trickled, while the narrow rills moved just enough water through the site to cool the air as it evaporated.

Water was also exploited for its reflective properties. At the seventeenth-century Taj Mahal, the effect of the already sublime dome and minarets of Shah Jahan's monument to grief is doubled in the reflective canal that leads to it. Likewise, in the Court of the Myrtles at the medieval Alhambra palace complex in Granada, the graceful arches of the courtyard are mirrored in the central pool.

The private, inward-facing garden patio is a particular feature of the Alhambra, whose courtyards, such as the Court of the Main Canal and Court of the Lions, were influential not just on gardens in the region but also through the ... ... right shown in ... ... rational patio gardens of 1960s Britain.

Islamic rulers were keen plantsmen, collecting plants and stocking their gardens with noteworthy specimens. In the royal gardens of Al-Andalus, renowned botanists, such as Ibn al-Wafid and Ibn Bassal, gardened and studied plants, and wrote influential treatises on botanic medicine and agriculture. The cultural cross-pollination of the *covivienca*

between Islamic, Christian and Jewish communities in Spain helped disseminate Islamic gardening know-how to medieval and Renaissance Europe, whose formal pleasure gardens can trace at least some of their DNA to the Islamic garden.

NURSERYMEN & SEEDSMEN

The trade in seeds and plants developed from the seventeenth century, with **DESIGN-AND-SUPPLY** *companies such as the Brompton Park Nursery in London shaping* **HORTICULTURAL TASTE**. *Mail-order plant and seed businesses* **BOOMED** *together with the railways in the nineteenth century, making seed merchants such as* **BURPEE** *in the US, and Thompson and Morgan in the UK, into* **HOUSEHOLD NAMES**.

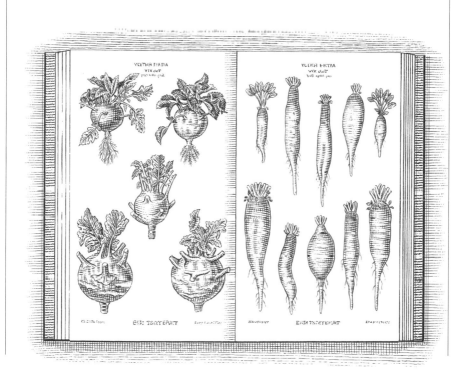

Even today, when practically any plant or seed is but a mouse click away, nursery and seed companies still print catalogues in large numbers. Lavishly colourful, they sell an irresistible horticultural fix of novelty and familiarity, and the promise of bumper crops of flowers and vegetables.

Such catalogues have a long track record; the oldest known example was published by Dutch bulb merchant Emanuel Sweerts in 1612. Colour printing technology in the nineteenth century coincided with the boom in hobby gardening, the growth of consumerism and the rise of rail transport: perfect conditions in which companies such as Suttons, Carters, and Thompson and Morgan could thrive and become nationally renowned businesses.

Then, as now, quality and reliability were key selling points. Before the mid-eighteenth century, when the first specialist seed shops appeared in London, seed was sold by pedlars and general stores. Low-grade merchandise was the bane of gardeners' lives; the aptly named Richard Gardiner, the author of a late sixteenth-century vegetable-growing manual, railed bitterly against the 'caterpillars' who traded in dud seeds.

Specialist seed merchants extolled the viability of their seeds, and protected their reputations from horticulturally inexperienced customers by providing cultivation instructions. These could be anything from idiot-proof guidance on the back of seed packets through to *The Blue Book of Gardening*, the comprehensive catalogue-cum-gardening manual published by Carters Seeds. Quality-conscious companies trialled their seeds in the field, and in 1840 Suttons Seeds established its own seed-testing laboratory; the company's reputation for quality being rewarded with a Royal Warrant in 1858.

The gardener's insatiable appetite for novelty encouraged innovation. Nurseries set their hybridizers to work and dispatched plant collectors around the world. Loddiges, an East London nursery founded in the eighteenth century, was famous for its exotic plants, and in the nineteenth century helped test the newly invented Wardian case. The Veitch Nurseries funded E. H. Wilson's plant-hunting trips to China in 1899 and 1903, while in the US, Burpee Seeds set up research facilities in Pennsylvania and in California, developing, among other things, Spencer sweet peas for the American climate, and breeding new vegetable varieties such as Iceberg lettuce (introduced 1894).

Now-familiar plants bear the names of the nursery that originated them; the Six Hills Nursery, near Stevenage, for example, is immortalized in their 1935 introduction *Nepeta* 'Six Hills Giant', while Jackman's (one of the many nurseries that set up in Surrey in the 1800s), introduced its large flowered hybrid *Clematis* 'Jackmanii' in 1862.

The scale of the pioneering nurseries was impressive; Brompton Park Nursery, the pre-eminent nursery of the late seventeenth and early eighteenth centuries, occupied at least 50 acres of prime South Kensington, with stock estimated to have run into millions of plants. In Berlin, the tree nursery established by Christoph Späth in 1720 covered 120 hectares. In the nineteenth century, both Loddiges and Späth nurseries had sufficient space and ambition to plant their own arboreta – Späth's survives today as part of Humboldt University. By the 1820s, Loddiges' exotic plants and technologically advanced hothouses had become a tourist destination, the Hackney Botanic Garden. Urbanization, however, eventually forced many historic nurseries to close or relocate – Loddiges shut in 1852 – paving the way for the out-of-town garden centre some 100 years later.

GUERRILLA GARDENING

These days, the once-subversive act of gardening other people's land is **CIVIL DISOBEDIENCE** *at its* **MOST CIVILIZED** *– twenty-first-century guerrilla gardeners are more likely to have their own* **WEBSITE***, have presented a TED talk, or featured in an* **ADVERTISING CAMPAIGN** *than they are to have spent a night in the cells for their troubles.*

It was not always thus. In spring 1649, in the ferment of the English Civil War, the Diggers (a group of radicals who viewed land as a 'common treasury for all') made several attempts to farm communally. By 1650 their settlements had been destroyed, but the Diggers' defiant cultivation of common land has resonated down the centuries.

Motives for guerrilla gardening vary. In July 1906 a group of unemployed men started to cultivate a patch of waste ground in East London to show their willingness to work. Their 'Plaistow Land Grab' attracted public sympathy but was short-lived: the squatters, who made a point of working full days, were evicted in August (although not before they had planted some Brussels sprouts and dug a 6-metre [20-foot] well).

In World War II London, many bombsites became extemporary gardens, coaxed from the rubble by off-duty city workers. Firewatchers created the garden on the bombed-out premises of the Goldsmiths'

Company on Gresham Street, which in 1950 was awarded 'Best Garden on a Blitzed Site', and is one of several bombsite gardens in the City of London still flourishing today.

In the early 1970s, New York City's illicit gardening scene played out against the backdrop of that era's financial crisis. In this landscape of homesteaded properties and political activism, the 'green guerrillas' led by Liz Christy cleared and planted a vacant lot on the corner of Bowery and Houston and created what became New York's first community garden.

Seed bombing, a favourite guerrilla tactic, has surprisingly genteel origins. In the 1880s, garden writer William Robinson reputedly threw bluebell seeds from the train while commuting from his Sussex home, creating the bluebell woods that attract tourists today. *Eryngium giganteum* 'Miss Willmott's Ghost' commemorates the eponymous Edwardian horticulturalist who would famously scatter its seeds in other people's gardens, leaving its spectral presence to appear the following year.

Today's aesthetically motivated guerrillas gentrify underfunded municipal streets with kerbside meadows and micro gardens in potholes. Unofficial gardens in newly prime areas are vulnerable to redevelopment, although some have dodged that bullet by becoming community gardens. Prinzessinnengarten, a productive organic enterprise started on leasehold wasteland in central Berlin in 2009, is containerized for ease of relocation.

Sustainable food is another guerrilla preoccupation, with open-harvest projects such as Ron Finley's 'gangsta garden' in South LA aiming to make fresh produce freely available to all. Reviving the Diggers' 'common treasury', guerrilla foragers graze on the urban forest, guided by online maps of street trees collated by groups such as Falling Fruit. Community-harvest groups tackle urban fruit gluts, turning would-be waste into preserves, while in San Francisco the Guerrilla Grafters graft fruit-bearing branches onto publicly accessible ornamental fruit trees to grow a harvest for all.

GURUS

From Pliny the Elder to Dr Hessayon's multi-million-selling **'EXPERT'** *guides, gardeners have long chosen to consult a* **HIGHER AUTHORITY** *in matters of practical gardening and taste.*

Twenty-first-century gardeners in a quandary are never more than a mouse click away from a pedagogic podcast or instant opinion. But horticultural hand-holding is nothing new – Roman writers such as Columella dispensed advice on gardening – and specialist books began to appear from the seventeenth century, reflecting both the emergence of a print industry and gardening as a fashionable hobby.

Some titles outlived their authors by decades, if not centuries. John Gerard's illustrated *Herball* was first published in 1597 but was still being consulted in the nineteenth century. Manuals such as Thomas Hill's *The Gardener's Labyrinth* (1577) and Leonard Meager's *The English Gardener* (1670) provided design ideas as well as practical advice; seasonal 'what to do when' guides, such as John Evelyn's *Gard'ner's Almanac* (1664), became a genre in itself.

Gardening literature boomed in the nineteenth century as the population became more literate – and garden obsessed. Magazines like *Amateur Gardening*, launched in 1884, catered for hands-on gardeners eager to learn about the latest plants and techniques from experts (a formula that the magazine continues to this day). And national newspapers started to carry gardening columns, rather belatedly, in the first decade of the twentieth century; after World War II, grandees such as Vita Sackville-West and Christopher Lloyd became horticultural tastemakers through their columns (for the *Observer* and *Guardian* respectively).

Gardening know-how was also disseminated over the airwaves. Cecil Henry Middleton began broadcasting his weekly *In Your Garden* BBC radio programme in 1934; his conversational yet authoritative style drew listeners in their millions and cemented his reputation as the 'most famous gardener since Adam'. A show featuring a panel of horticultural experts (*How Does Your Garden Grow?*) then followed in 1947; in 1958 it was renamed *Gardeners' Question Time* and given Middleton's Sunday afternoon slot. To date, its panel has answered over 30,000 questions posed by the gardening public.

'Mr Middleton' presented the BBC's first television gardening show in 1936, but TV gardening did not get going properly until after the war. *Gardeners' World* launched in 1968 and conferred household-name status on its presenters from Percy Thrower onwards, as well as immortalizing their gardens. Its presenter between 1979 and 1996, Geoff Hamilton, is credited with popularizing organic gardening – a measure of the programme's clout.

The internet is the latest go-to guru, offering advice from well-informed bloggers and authorities like the RHS. When the 'world's favourite gardening writer' Dr D. G. Hessayon announced his retirement in 2013, he cited the internet as the reason. Admittedly, Hessayon might justifiably have felt his work was done, having sold over 50 million books since launching *Be Your Own Garden Expert* in 1958. His hugely successful 'Expert' titles provide amateur gardeners with straightforward and concise instruction, covering areas of particular interest such as lawns, roses and houseplants. With an estimated half of all British households owning one of his books, Hessayon's influence (like that of Gerard before him) is likely to endure for some years yet.

PUBLIC PARKS

Rapid **URBANIZATION** *in the nineteenth century made freely accessible* **RECREATIONAL SPACES** *a priority for city authorities. Drawing their initial inspiration from the* **SWEEPING PARKLAND** *of English country estates, Victorian city parks developed a style of their own.*

In London, Vauxhall Pleasure Gardens offered some scope for recreation among its wooded groves and allées, and public access was allowed in some royal parks (Hyde Park was opened to the public in the seventeenth century, as was the Tuileries garden in Paris), but until the mid-nineteenth century, opportunities for outdoor leisure were scarce for the urban working classes.

Public pressure for healthy open spaces prompted a drive to create purpose-built 'people's parks'. Derby Arboretum was one of the earliest, commissioned by local industrialist Joseph Strutt and designed by John Loudon to offer the city's inhabitants 'an opportunity of enjoying with their families, exercise and recreation in the fresh air'. It opened in September 1840, but charged for entrance on all but two days a week, unlike the government-sponsored Victoria Park in London's East End, which opened in 1845 with free entry to all. Birkenhead Park, in Merseyside, followed two years later with an influential design by Joseph Paxton, the Duke of Devonshire's hyper-talented head gardener.

With its *rus-in-urbe* layout of carriage drives, pedestrian walks, grassy expanses, picturesque clumps of trees and naturalistic serpentine lakes, counterbalanced by more intimate and formal garden spaces, Birkenhead Park became a template for many municipal parks, including Central Park in New York, whose 'Greensward' design by Frederick Law Olmsted and Calvert Vaux incorporated Paxtonian ideas such as separating equestrian and pedestrian traffic, following Olmsted's visit to England in 1850.

Rockeries, palm houses and other haute gardening accoutrements also found their way into parks, for the enjoyment and edification of the populace. Carpet bedding displays were popular from the 1860s and, continuing long after the fashion had abated in private gardens, became synonymous with municipal planting schemes. Battersea Park was known for its tropical and subtropical plants, while for many years at Victoria Park – true to its founding principles – spare bedding plants were given to the local population. At the turn of the century, under the auspices of J. J. Sexby, the first superintendent of London's parks, several of the capital's parks, Brockwell and Ravenscourt among them, acquired fashionable Arts and Crafts-style 'Olde English Gardens'.

As organized sports became increasingly popular, parks added cricket pitches, tennis courts, swimming pools and boating ponds to their offering. Parks were convenient venues for international exhibitions; Olmsted and Vaux's Jackson Park in Chicago hosted the 1893 World's Fair, while the modern-day pleasure gardens installed in Battersea Park for the 1951 Festival of Britain drew some 8 million visitors.

Despite severe funding pressures, parks continue to evolve in the twenty-first century, with new parks such as the High Line in New York (from 2009) and the Allain Provost-designed Birmingham Eastside City Park (opened 2013) moving away from the English landscape park tradition to fully embrace their urban surroundings, and reflect new ideas about sustainability.

LOW-MAINTENANCE
GARDENS

The holy grail of many a **TIME-POOR** *modern gardener, low- or no-maintenance gardens tend to favour* **HARD LANDSCAPING** *over soft, but* **WHO ARE THEY KIDDING**? *Real gardening is all about* **PLANTS** *and getting your* **HANDS DIRTY**.

Although sun, soil, air and water are usually cited as the essential requirements for a successful garden, time and money come in quite handy as well. When these two commodities are in short supply, a low-maintenance approach might be a necessary evil, since the sight of a much-loved garden turning feral can be hard to bear.

Low-maintenance gardens have come a long way since the ground-cover-and-shrub

combos of the 1960s and 70s. Gardening organizations such as the RHS now advise on 'lower input solutions', with tips on designing your garden to suit your lifestyle, replacing lawns with paving or artificial grass, planting easy-care shrubs instead of high-maintenance flower borders, or simply learning to have lower standards. Other time- and energy-saving strategies include using weed-suppressing membranes and mulches, and a sensible 'right plant in the right place' policy (bulbs are often recommended for low-maintenance schemes, obligingly flowering year after year once they have been planted).

Thanks to technology, paradise does not always need to be paved; robotic lawnmowers can be set to work on lawns, while programmable irrigation systems take the tedium out of watering, allowing even the most committed gardener the possibility of a summer holiday. Chemicals, once seen as miraculous time-savers, are now not widely recommended, but can achieve rapid results when weeds and pests threaten to get the upper hand.

Ironically, the garden features being replaced today in the name of an easy life were themselves once the low-maintenance option. When the fashion for carpet bedding faded in the nineteenth century, formality gave way to a more relaxed approach, with romantically inclined Arts and Crafts herbaceous borders. The development of the lawnmower having made grass-care easier, super-intensive carpet beds were grassed over – an echo of how, a century earlier, the grassy parkland and specimen trees of the English landscape movement replaced the manicured parterres and plats of Baroque gardens.

Grass was again the go-to low-maintenance solution in the belt-tightening aftermath of the world wars. Austerity, a lack of gardeners and changing fashions saw labour-intensive walled kitchen gardens being grassed over, turned into swimming pools or tennis courts, or, the ultimate low-maintenance solution, simply abandoned. Herbaceous borders that were deemed too demanding were downgraded to mixed borders, reverted to shrubbery or – fescue to the rescue again – laid to lawn.

Low maintenance is a relative concept – one person's meditative mowing session is another's weekly torture, and abundant borders can be seen either as a source of anxiety or pleasure. For those with money but no time, hiring help might be the most satisfactory 'lower-input solution'; with horticulture an increasingly popular first or second career choice, there are now more gardeners available to take the strain.

GARDEN RESTORATION

Garden restoration has become more **COMMONPLACE** *over the past*
30 years, with gardens increasingly being valued as **CULTURALLY**
IMPORTANT *art works meriting significant* **CAPITAL INVESTMENT**.

Ephemeral creations at the best of times, gardens are vulnerable to changing horticultural taste and neglect; in a sense, all gardens are in constant need of restoration, hence the gardener's refrain: 'You should have been here last week'.

Sometimes even yesterday is too late; the 'Great Storm' of October 1987 felled millions of trees across southern England overnight. Initially seen as a disaster, the aftermath of the storm became the catalyst for renovation projects at historic gardens such as Nymans in Sussex, whose Pinetum has been restored using young trees propagated from fallen specimens. At Kew, which lost 700 trees in the storm, upended specimens revealed compacted soil and fatally shallow root systems, a discovery that ushered in new tree-management strategies.

Self contained and relatable, walled kitchen gardens have been particularly popular subjects for restoration. The 'lost' gardens of Heligan, rediscovered in ruinous condition in 1990, were restored and opened to the public as a memorial to the gardeners who worked there on the eve of World War I. The National Trust has restored 30 out of its portfolio of 140 walled gardens, returning many, like Attingham Park, to productivity.

Gardens can 'disappear' in a remarkably short space of time; those revitalizing gardens made in the nineteenth or twentieth centuries usually have the benefit of contemporary documentation to consult. The 1970s restoration of the formal gardens designed at Hestercombe in Somerset by Edwin Lutyens and Gertrude Jekyll was guided by the fortuitous discovery of some of Jekyll's original plans in the potting shed.

Where gardens have disappeared without visible trace, archaeological spadework can determine the location of features hard and soft, pinpointing even the position of planting pits, such as the topiaries that once stood in William III's Privy Garden at Hampton Court, which was restored in the 1990s.

At complex sites, such as Wrest Park, modern non-invasive technologies such as aerial lidar and geophysical surveys have been used to trace the Grade I-listed garden's hidden 300-year history, rediscovering the layout of early eighteenth-century parterres, and a Capability Brown parkscape. Old-fashioned aerial photography (courtesy of a Luftwaffe reconnaissance mission) revealed the lost garden at Lyveden New Bield, created by the Catholic recusant Sir

Thomas Tresham in the 1500s, and complete with labyrinth and orchard. Tresham's letters, written from prison, were an additional source for the restoration, and detailed his intentions for the garden, right down to specific fruit varieties.

American designer Beatrix Farrand future-proofed the garden she designed at Dumbarton Oaks by anticipating the decisions that subsequent gardeners would have to make. Covering every eventuality, from pruning to plant replacement, her handbook for the garden, *The Plant Book for Dumbarton Oaks*, ensured that her vision for the garden remained intact after its transfer to Harvard University in 1941.

Before

After

GARDENING
MAGAZINES

—ᴍᴍ—

First developed at the end of the eighteenth century,
periodical publications were ideally suited to the
SEASONAL NATURE *of gardening. The ensuing*
glut of gardening magazines and newspapers reflected
both the **POPULARITY OF GARDENING** *as*
a hobby and the increasing professionalism of the
HORTICULTURAL INDUSTRY.

Britain's first illustrated gardening periodical, *The Botanical Magazine*, was founded in 1787 by the Quaker botanist William Curtis, and survives to this day as *Curtis's Botanical Magazine*. With its focus on 'ornamental foreign plants', *Curtis's Botanical Magazine* was snapped up by a readership eager to discover the latest horticultural discoveries. Plants were described using the new-fangled Linnaean system, and illustrated with hand-coloured prints by leading botanic artists.

Botanical publishing quickly became a competitive marketplace. Rivals included *The Botanical Register*, set up in 1815 by Sydenham Edwards, a disgruntled former artist on *The Botanical Magazine*, and *The Botanical Cabinet* produced by Loddiges nursery. Sumptuously illustrated by George Cooke, the *Cabinet*'s connoisseurial subscribers included the botanist Sir Joseph Banks.

At the other end of the market, niche titles catered for working-class hobby growers

or 'florists'; the first issue of *The Floricultural Cabinet* magazine in 1833 made a point of reassuring its readers that 'the greatest simplicity in expression will be attended to; so that each article may be clearly understood'. Professional gardeners, too, could consult their own publications. *The Gardeners' Magazine*, launched by John Claudius Loudon in 1826, catered to 'practical' gardeners, with news of the latest plants and improving educational articles alongside notices of plant sales and advertisements. Loudon's high-minded venture was unable to compete with cheaper rival titles, though, and his magazine died along with him in 1843.

The Gardeners' Chronicle, started by John Lindley and Joseph Paxton in 1841, proved more resilient. A respectable paper for working gardeners, the *Chronicle* desired to be 'the gardener's friend; collecting what is useful to him, opposing wrong, defending right'; it continues today as *Horticulture Week*. Its content ranged widely, from appraisals of the latest fruit and vegetable varieties, to opinion pieces by luminaries such as Sir Joseph Hooker, and the previous week's weather report.

Another hardy perennial periodical, *Amateur Gardening*, launched in 1884 and is still going strong. Its first editor, Shirley Hibberd, was an expert on town gardens who used his own plot in Stoke Newington as an experimental ground, sharing his findings with his readers very much in the way gardening correspondents do today.

As well as transmitting hands-on gardening know-how, magazines provided a mouthpiece for leading tastemakers. *The Garden* and *Gardening Illustrated*, both started by William Robinson in the 1870s, promoted his 'wild' gardening approach with pieces by like-minded contributors, like William Morris and Gertrude Jekyll. Jekyll also wrote for *Country Life*, which regularly featured the country residences whose enviable gardens she had designed.

Two world wars reshaped the modern gardening magazine. *Homes and Gardens* was launched in 1919 and addressed middle-class aspirations with a focus on practical design and labour-saving devices. *Vogue*'s *House & Garden* launched in 1947 and expressed the country's yearning to rebuild domestic life after the destruction of World War II. In its first issue, designer Russell Page set the course for post-war gardeners, encouraging them to consider their gardens (in a way that we take for granted now), as 'an extension of the house – an outdoor room furnished as a floral library'.

INDEX

෴